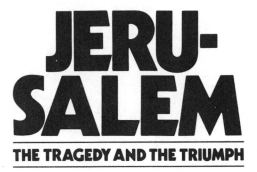

JERU-SALEM

THE TRAGEDY AND THE TRIUMPH

BOOKS BY CHARLES GULSTON

AND THE DREAMING
SOUTH AFRICAN POETRY: A NEW ANTHOLOGY
  (Joint Editor)
NO GREATER HERITAGE: THE TRIUMPHANT
  PROGRESS OF THE ABIDING WORD
ETERNITY IS FOR EVERYMAN
JERUSALEM: THE TRAGEDY AND THE TRIUMPH

JERU-SALEM

THE TRAGEDY AND THE TRIUMPH

CHARLES GULSTON

ZONDERVAN PUBLISHING HOUSE OF THE ZONDERVAN CORPORATION GRAND RAPIDS, MICHIGAN 49506

JERUSALEM: THE TRAGEDY AND THE TRIUMPH
© 1978 by The Zondervan Corporation
Grand Rapids, Michigan

Second printing August 1978

Library of Congress Cataloging in Publication Data

Gulston, Charles.
  Jerusalem: the tragedy and the triumph.

  Bibliography: p.
  Includes index.
  1. Jerusalem—History.   I. Title.

DS109.9.G84   956.94'4   77-21982
ISBN 0-310-35510-9

Printed in the United States of America

Acknowledgments

Werner Braun (4, 5, 7 [all in color section]); *British Museum* (76); *Carta, The Israel Map and Publishing Company* (31, 38, 81, 84, 88, 92 [top], 98, 110, 112, 123, 147, 160 [two], 166, 168, 178, 180 [bottom], 190, 200, 202, 221, 222, 248); *Central Zionist Archives* (210 [top], 216 [bottom]); *Gaalyah Cornfeld* (1 [color section], 26, 44, 52, 64, 70, 74, 92 [bottom], 104, 126, 134, 150 [bottom], 177, 180 [top left], 192, 224 [bottom], 258); *Historical Picture Service* (13, 89, 142, 157); *Imperial War Museum, London* (216 [top]); *Israel Department of Antiquities and Museums* (46); *Israel Government Press Office* (16, 28, 32, 34 [four], 40, 100 [top], 106, 118, 150 [top], 186 [two], 224 [top], 230, 234, 236 [two], 240, 242 [two], 250 [two]);*Israel State Archives* (180[top right]); *Keren Hayesod, United Israel Appeal, Photo Archives* (22 [three], 100 [bottom]); *Matson Photo Service* (58 [two], 210 [bottom], 266, 272); *Palphot* (2, 8 [both in color section]); *Frank Raymond* (3, 6 [both in color section]).

Contents

Part III

THE FINAL DAWN

Illustrations

MAPS

Preface

NO CITY IN THE WORLD is more symbolic of a people than Jerusalem. The tragedy and the miracle, the mystery and the paradox that are so much a part of Jewish history are all mirrored with a terrible clarity in the city of Zion.

Within recent years Jerusalem has emerged from comparative obscurity to the center, at times, of the international scene. As part of a predetermined saga, she had to be the metropolis once more of a reborn Israel. The land that had withered and died had to be inhabited and restored by a people who reentered the comity of nations as a creative force and fully independent state. The Hebrew prophets take the matter even further — to the final interlocking of Jewish and Gentile history with its cataclysmic consequences.

In her autobiography Golda Meir, prime minister of Israel from 1969 to 1974, states:

> From the time I came to Palestine as a young woman we have been forced to choose between what is more dangerous and what is less dangerous for us . . . and we are still in that situation or perhaps in an even graver one . . . To those who ask: "What of the future?" I still have only one answer: I believe that we will have peace with our neighbours, but I am sure that no one will make peace with a weak Israel. If Israel is not strong there will be no peace.[1]

This is true. But has the Jew been brought thus far for no other reason than that his land might be the storm center of the world? Is this to be the overriding sequel to his return from the "graveyards" of the nations? And will the strength (which is relative) of Israel always be a guarantee of peace? Courageous, determined, and well-

---

[1]Golda Meir, *My Life* (London: Weidenfeld & Nicolson, 1975), p. 387.

armed as she undoubtedly is, will these assets always save her? Put simply, is there no point to her national and territorial restoration other than that she might always be a target for attack?

At this stage in Jewish history, and particularly since the Yom Kippur War of 1973, such questions would not seem out of place. But one cannot begin to speculate on the future of a politically resurrected Israel without taking cognizance of the city that is her capital again after 2,500 years and without trying to discover, perhaps, the ultimate object of its repossession by a "peculiar people," and to what the sensational and sometimes miraculous events of the last half-century are really leading.

Again, one cannot think of Israel's future without realizing that Jerusalem is not just another city, but a unique creation, and that "to touch her," as Disraeli said of Palestine, "is to touch eternity." In so doing, one may perhaps see, as well, her destiny as the terminal of history.

For the Jew, the road back has been long and hard. But he has had to travel it because what began in Jerusalem must end there. One day the throne must replace the cross, the crown of gold the crown of thorns, the glory the infamy, the triumph the tragedy. And when the Beloved City surmounts its last crisis, it will be given, in the words of Isaiah, "beauty for ashes, and the oil of joy for mourning . . . when the Lord of hosts shall reign in Mount Zion, and in Jerusalem, and before his ancients gloriously, the moon will be confounded and the sun ashamed" (Isa. 61:3; 24:23).

Toward this climax Jerusalem is moving. To recall a little of what has taken place along the way may not, perhaps, be unrewarding.

11

PART I
The Gathering Dusk

All that pass by clap their hands at thee; they hiss and wag their head at the daughter of Jerusalem, saying, Is this the city that men call the perfection of beauty, the joy of the whole earth? — Lamentations 2:15

1
On The Judean Hills

THERE IS A ROAD that winds upward for some thirty miles from the eastern shores of the Mediterranean to a city that once was confined to a small but formidable cluster of hills. Today it has spread far beyond its original boundaries. But it is still not a large city compared with other capitals of the world, nor in the modern conception of the term could it be called important. In fact, by all human reckoning, it should not be there at all.

Like Ur of the Chaldees and Babylon of old, it should have become, long ago, but a heap of stones and the habitation of owls. Even its name, at one time, was changed in an attempt to obliterate it from memory. But the Empire under which that happened has itself vanished, and from the dust and ashes of its innumerable destructions Jerusalem continued to rise, a strange and challenging phenomenon in man's history.

It was a city that had to survive.

Why?

Looking back from this vantage point in time, we find that the answer is plain enough. Jerusalem had to survive its first 1,000 years so that it could be the stage for the central act of all time. It is quite clear now that it had to continue to exist, despite the onslaughts of the most powerful nations of the day. In the light of subsequent events, there was never any question of the pagan plunderers from Assyria and Babylonia laying Jerusalem waste forever. It was not in the scheme of things that they should.

Nor when the scepter of world power passed from Greece to Rome was there any immediate reduction of the Jewish capital. Though Pompey razed the walls, killed 12,000 of its inhabitants, and

17

entered the Holy of Holies in the temple, he did not destroy the city. But history was then moving towards its supreme crisis. And Jerusalem stood poised and proud, tragically blind to the immense significance of the choice it was to make — one that was to bring calamity to itself but deliverance and blessing to the rest of mankind. The hour had arrived when it was to put to death the Light of the World, and then to perish itself in the holocaust He had foretold.

"Verily I say unto thee, there shall not be left one stone upon another that shall not be thrown down" was the fate predicted for the sanctuary that Herod had built in order to find favor with his Jewish subjects. It is not surprising that these words sounded strange at the time they were uttered. The temple was an architectural masterpiece. Many of its blocks of stones weighed one hundred tons and more. But in less than forty years the prophecy was fulfilled to the letter. Not only the temple but Jerusalem lay in ruins and the Roman general Titus had added his name to the growing list of the city's desolators.

Words have failed to describe adequately the suffering of a people in this episode in history. Though high and isolated on its rocky pedestal, the city that had defied an Empire in the heyday of its power was reduced to a smoldering shell at the end of perhaps the most horrifying siege ever endured.

But it was not the end, either for a nation or its metropolis. The Jerusalem of the Hebrew kings, the City of David, had fallen for the last time. Already, however, a new age had begun. The seeds of Christianity had been firmly planted beside the very roots of Judaistic beliefs. Other Jerusalems were to rise, still on the ancient site. But they would have no temple, and their streets would run with blood as new conquerors sought to place the Cross or the Crescent on their respective shrines. Or they would know long periods of obscurity, years when they would lie forgotten, almost, by the changing world around them.

But the city was always there, ready to emerge from the shadows. Seemingly remote, it would suddenly burst into sharp focus, the center once more of significant and, more than likely, turbulent events.

Whatever the nature, however, of the catastrophes that have engulfed Jerusalem during the past 1,900 years, one thing was never in doubt — its survival. And again it is possible to see why. As the twentieth century advanced, it had to be there so that a people could be drawn irresistibly back to it from the four corners of the earth, and the oft-repeated hope, "next year in Jerusalem," fulfilled at last. It had to become the fulcrum of the new state.

And as the rich, crop-bearing plain falls away and the ascent to the Israeli capital steepens, you see it, suddenly, overflowing into the valleys and the harsh Judean hills, far beyond the walls of ancient Zion and those of Suleiman the Magnificent.

There have been changes here, of course, since a Man stood trial in Pilate's judgment hall, and the streets outside rang with the cry, "Crucify Him, crucify Him!" But enough remains to cause the stranger who appears today before Jerusalem's open gates to tremble a little, conscious that it is indeed no ordinary city to which he has come.

2
The Supreme Paradox

IT HAS BEEN SAID that if blood were indelible, Old Jerusalem would be red, all red. The words, weighed against the stark facts of history, appall in their degree of accuracy. But of course the city is not red. The sun and the rain have erased the scarlet stains. It is tawny-colored, "the colour of a lion skin," as H. V. Morton describes it. It is different from the new city only because the centuries have weathered the local sandstone more, particularly portions of the ancient walls.

And there is perhaps no other experience quite like seeing these for the first time. In some strange way it is these crenelated, golden gray ramparts that epitomize more than anything else, the past in a land where antiquity abounds. That they are less than 450 years old doesn't really matter. One feels that it was walls like these that Nehemiah restored when the exiles returned from Babylon, that kept, for incredible periods, the Roman Legions at bay, and down upon which Christ often gazed from the Mount of Olives.

There is something awesome and indefinably evocative about these fortifications. They rear in subtle arrogance over road and ravine, rows of tombstones and modern highways, potent in their mesmerism, as if their very stones would speak. And if they did, would lay bare a city's soul.

It is here at the walls of Old Jerusalem that the past and present meet as they do nowhere else in quite the same way. Northward and westward flows the new city, gleaming in its coat of sandstone, vibrant with the life that quickens and sustains a thriving metropolis of 300,000 inhabitants. On every side the earth bears witness to a mighty transformation. Here the descendants of those who "wept by the rivers of Babylon" (Ps. 137:1) have built their twentieth-century "citadel" with its House of Parliament, its university, research laboratories, and vast apartment blocks. Here a nation has erected memorials to its war dead, its martyrs and its modern prophets. Here have been planted roots that it has been vowed will never again be plucked up.

David sang of Jerusalem "as a city that is compact together" (Ps. 122:3). But no longer does it answer to that description. For it now straddles the virgin hills beyond the walls that once enclosed it and the barbed-wire barricades that divided it in its modern agony, but it is compacted together in a new sense now in that a "no-man's land" no longer cuts the city in two, and to pass through what was once the Mandelbaum Gate is no longer to enter the territory of another people. There are no "frontiers" now in Jerusalem. Two halves have become a single unit, though centuries separate them in visible aspects.

Behind its two and a half miles of lofty ramparts, Old Jerusalem slumbers on, almost impervious, it would seem, to the passing of time. Even the ceaseless roar of traffic on the encircling highways does not disturb it. Only the low murmur of voices and the shuffle or tread of feet break the silence of the narrow souks, the sacred shrines and churches, the great paved platform of the temple site now dominated by the Dome of the Rock and the El Aqsa mosque, or the crowded precincts of the Wailing Wall.

It is not easy to believe that modern warfare has come here, for its scars have healed, and there is little to remind one of a world in turmoil outside the ancient walls. Pass through the Damascus Gate from the bus- and taxi-congested road that leads to Jericho and the centuries vanish. One feels suddenly conscious of having begun a long journey back in time. The paradox that is Jerusalem fades into the shadows and the dark recesses of its tortuous alleyways, the beauty and the quiet of some of its sanctuaries.

Instead, you remember, if you are a believer, only that the Prince of Peace died here, and that the full significance of this is beyond human comprehension. Only from a distance, and in retrospect, does the other side of the picture take shape. Stretching back to Abraham, there emerges the portrait of a city unique in its vicissitude of fortunes, its fury and its violence, its perfidy and its glory. And in contemplating a historical record that never fails to amaze and mystify, there comes also the realization that it was on a hill outside these walls that violence climbed to its most awful height. When man put to death the Son of Man, God hid the deed from human eyes for three hours. Nothing could ever again equal the terribleness and monstrous iniquity of that act. Yet in it lay the secret and means of man's redemption.

For this supreme paradox Jerusalem was chosen before the worlds began. To the shadow of her high walls, one day, a donkey would come carrying the hope of the world. A city would open its gates in welcome and a people would shout hosannas to their King. Zechariah (9:9) described the colorful event five hundred years before it happened. But the rider of the ass was not deceived by the acclaim of the multitude that day, for He knew that soon the cry of those same people would be a vastly different one.

But it was not because of what He knew would happen to Himself that Jesus of Nazareth wept that day outside the walls of Jerusalem. It was over a city that knew how to kill its prophets and stone those sent to it, whose final act of rejection was to leave it desolate, both spiritually and materially, whose enemies "would lay it even with the ground" (Luke 19:44).

The Jerusalem that Jesus knew was to pass, more thoroughly than any of its predecessors. But what happened in the lee of its protective ramparts was to be remembered for the rest of time. It was to become, indeed, the arbiter of man's destiny. And we go today to see, if we can, the place where the cross once stood. Whether we are satisfied with what we are shown does not matter. What does matter is that an event took place somewhere in the environs of this city that divided history in two and linked Jerusalem forever with the fate of all mankind.

The southeastern corner of the Temple Mount.

3
The Beloved Olivet

Old Moslem cemetery (foreground), Mount of Olives, and Garden of Geth-semane.

WHEN THE SUN begins to set over the Judean hills, the Old City of Jerusalem falls into shadow. But across the deep Kidron Valley on the east, a hill always catches the dying rays of sunlight. Lining its summit are a variety of Christian shrines, and a luxury hotel now caps its southern extremity. Down its slopes straggles the oldest Jewish cemetery in the world and near its base a clump of olive and cyprus trees allegedly mark the place where a garden called Geth-semane once existed.

For those who visit Jerusalem for some external confirmation of their faith, it is this hill that invariably stirs the emotions. For the Mount of Olives still stands as in the days of Christ's humanity, basically unaltered, just as a lake in Galilee remains as it was when fishermen suddenly left their nets one day and began a new life.

To gaze on these is to gaze on authentic evidence of things long ago. Here in his ardor for preserving the past man has not been able to create a spectacle merely of disillusionment. It is possible, as the light fades also from this hill, to conjure up those incidents in the Life for which it was the setting. This was the place that Jesus seemed to love, where He found peace and was able to pray in solitude, where "he was wont to abide at night." But it was also here that He was in great agony of spirit, here that He was betrayed, and the paradox that is Jerusalem stretches, it would seem, to the slopes of Olivet. For the earth that felt the tread of feet "shod with the preparation of the gospel of peace" has also resounded with the tramp of men prepared for war.

The tactical significance of this rounded ridge of cretaceous limestone is immediately apparent, for it rises some 250 feet above the walls of the Old City. From this vantage point the Roman Legions under Titus looked down on the city they were going to destroy. Other armies have camped on its slopes, some not so long ago. It was on a Wednesday in June 1,897 years after Titus, that a colonel in the Israeli army was given orders to begin his assault on Jerusalem from the summit of the Mount of Olives. Just before nine o'clock that morning, Israeli armor smashed through St. Stephen's Gate, and a few minutes later Colonel Motta Gur was standing on the temple site. For the first time in 780 years — since its occupation by Saladin — the muezzin's call to prayer was not heard in Jerusalem. It was to sound again but control of a city had passed back into the hands of a "peculiar people" after 2,553 years. The wheel had turned full cycle since Nebuchadnezzar first crushed their sovereignty in 586 B.C.

It was perhaps on the Mount of Olives that Nebuchadnezzar pitched his camp, his soldiers using the trees on hand to light it at night. And as darkness spreads over the hillside now, the first lights to appear are those from the sprawling trespasser on the southern spur.

But others quickly follow, dispelling the blackness with, one feels, an incongruous artificiality. For it was here that the Lord of heaven went back to heaven, and lights shine out from edifices supposedly marking the site of the Ascension. That they may not be geographically exact does not matter. All that matters is that His disciples saw Jesus borne out of their sight. And then they heard the promise that He would come again "in like manner." It is enough to know that from somewhere on the hilltop that He loved Christ went back to the glory He had temporarily relinquished, having accomplished His appointed task.

Olivet has always been there, "a Sabbath-day's journey from Jerusalem," watcher over the ever-changing scene below her, sometimes participator in the tragic drama being enacted. When the city fell, and the conquerors with the conquered departed, it remained. It knew that one day the exiles would return. There would be new walls, and another city would rise on Mount Zion. It knew, too, one day the Son of Man would find shelter on its slopes and "be betrayed there into the hands of sinful men." It knew itself chosen, like the city beneath it, as an instrument in the divine plan of things.

Patiently it awaits now the climax to its long vigil: the day it will cleave in two, and a great valley divide its north part from its south. It will be when all nations will be gathered against Jerusalem.

It is not a small thing to watch a day die on the Mount of Olives. For you will have seen a great place. You will have seen the place where the Savior of the world was taken up to heaven in a cloud, the part of earth to which He will return in the fullness of time.

Looking east. Basilica of the Agony in the Garden of Gethsemane.

Looking from the southeast to west, Basilica of the Agony at the foot of the Mount of Olives.

4
The Wailing Wall

Clockwise: Jews at Western Wall, man praying at Western Wall, some of the equipment inside the Náhal Sorek Atomic Research Center, and the exterior of the Atomic Research Center.

NOTHING, ONE FEELS, is impossible in Israel. It is the land of modern miracles, where, during the past fifty years the waste places have been inhabited and the desert made to yield up its treasures. The valleys and the plains are sown to beyond where the eye can see: great forests of Jerusalem pine, the tamarisk, and the eucalyptus clothe the once stark hills. In green and lovely Galilee, on the coastal Plain of Sharon, the harvests are waiting to be reaped.

But what of the south, for centuries in bondage to the pitiless Negev? Here too, there is a blooming of its own. Near where Abraham dug his wells at Beersheba, nuclear power is purifying salt water. No longer is this the kingdom of the Bedouin and his black tents of goat hair. What once was a shadowy dot in the shifting sands is now a thriving capital bursting at the seams with new citizens of an infant state.

The desert is being forced to retreat.

Farther east, deep down in a great hollow of the earth, where the cities of Sodom and Gomorrah perished in a "rain of fire and brimstone," factories are boosting the economy of a nation with rich deposits from a vast, but slowly shrinking lake. Between the heights of Golan and the desolate mountains of Moab, a "brave new world" is making phenomenal efforts to exist.

And belonging to it now, and in its very center, is the segment of a Wall, some sixty yards long by twenty yards high in which tufts of grass are growing in the crevices between the massive stones. To it there comes a ceaseless stream of solemn-faced petitioners. This was conquest's richest gain in 1967 and a prize from which a people have vowed they will never again be parted. Jerusalem may have more spectacular sights to offer than this, but nothing stranger. It is one that haunts the memory.

You cannot forget the large square — cleared after the Six-Day War of debris and old houses — in front of the ancient masonry with a low partition in the center separating the sexes; the black-clad figures rocking to and fro and nodding their heads in compliance with the injunction of the Psalmist: "All my bones shall say, O Lord, who is like unto thee" (Ps. 35:10); the silence that is broken only by the low murmur of voices intoning the Scriptures; the devout thrusting their petitions written on little pieces of paper into the cracks in the Wall, from which, it is held, Jehovah has never withdrawn His presence.

You remember that to the left of the open space and in a subterranean structure, you looked down a shaft and saw another fourteen tiers of 2,000-year-old stones that excavations have laid bare. The electric lights illuminating them seemed quite incongruous with the surroundings. Not even pictures are allowed to be taken within these precincts on the Sabbath when the Orthodox Jews, bearded, and in long black cloaks and fur-edged velvet caps, turn up in force. But the picture lives in the mind. And you remember wondering what it all meant and how it all started.

Ironically enough, it began with someone for whom the Jews shed no tears — Herod the Great. It was the temple built by Herod, magnificent in every way, that Titus laid level with the ground except for a remnant of the great retaining wall on the west. It was to this that a subject people began to cling as the years of exile and persecution began. Only this was left to remind them of a city and a sanctuary that had been unique. And so they had drifted slowly back to the ruins of Jerusalem, mourning a departed glory, until one day even this pilgrimage came to an end. A new city had begun to rise on the ancient site, called Aelia Capitolina, in honor of its planner, the Emperor Publius Aelius Hadrianus, whose passion for building ranks second only to Herod among the ancients.

It was a pagan city, built square like every Roman colony. Occupying the sacred temple site was a shrine to Jupiter and a statue of Hadrian, and it was this perhaps, more than anything else, that set the final revolt of the Jews under Bar Kochba in 134, in motion. It was crushed as mercilessly as the one launched seventy years before and Aelia Capitolina became a forbidden city to the people who, for 1,000 years, had lived where it was now standing. For nearly two centuries no Jew wept at the Western Wall.

Then came a relaxation of the ban. Pilgrimage to the relic was allowed once a year, on the ninth of August — the fateful day that saw the destruction of the temple, first by the Babylonians in 587 B.C. and then by the Romans exactly 657 years later. Even then the privilege had sometimes to be bought from unscrupulous sentries, prompting Jerome to remark that "they who once bought the blood of Messiah now buy their own tears." And legend holds that at night the massive stones of this defense rampart of the temple are covered with dew, tears that the Wailing Wall sheds with all Israel. In time, the new name given to the Roman colony was forgotten, but the Wall remained down the ages, a strange, unchanging source of inspiration in an ever-changing world.

Then in 1948 history repeated itself. For nineteen years after the birth of the new state of Israel another adversary stood within the gates of the Old City, and this time there was no concession regarding the Wall. It remained deserted — until that historic Wednesday of June 7, 1967, when General Narkiss achieved what he failed to do in 1948, and the significant notes of the Shofar echoed across the temple mount soon after ten o'clock in the morning.

There were tears of joy that day at the Western Wall. A relic, clothed with its aura of sanctity, had been won back, and was now part of a new Israel. But was there not still something missing in that great hour of triumph? Where was their sanctuary? There was possession of the temple site, but the "status quo" was to remain, creating a situation charged with irony.

Not even victory in the Six-Day War had been capable of ending a period of isolation from the sacred area that began over 1,800 years ago when Hadrian built an altar there to a Roman god. In the heart of Israel's modern kingdom of 30,000 square miles there is a foreign enclave of some thirty-five acres in which stand two Muslim shrines, one of them on the spot where Solomon built the first temple. The enclave lies adjacent to the Western Wall, steeped in a history as momentous, almost, as that of Jerusalem itself.

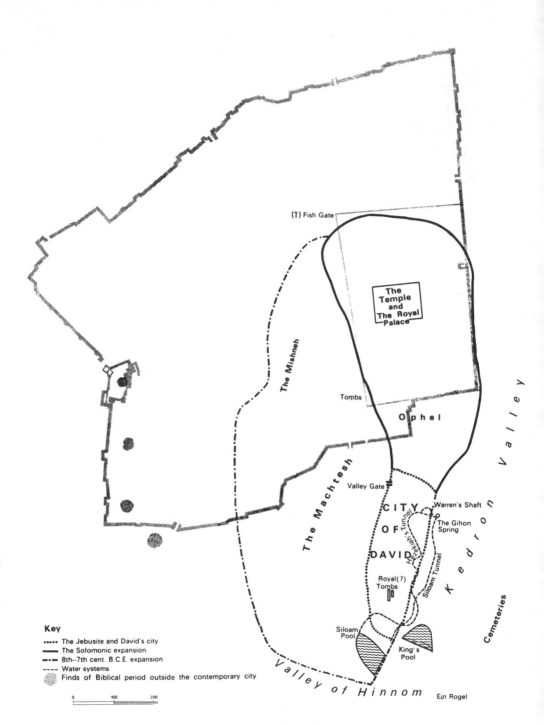

Jerusalem in the Canaanite, Jebusite, and Israelite periods (to 586 B.C.).

(?) Fish Gate

The
Temple
and
The Royal
Palace

The Mishneh

Tombs

O p h e l

The Machtesh

Valley Gate

Warren's Shaft

C I T Y

The Gihon
Spring

O F

D A V I D

Hezekiah's Tunnel

Siloam Tunnel

Royal(?)
Tombs

K e d r o n   V a l l e y

C e m e t e r i e s

Siloam
Pool

King's
Pool

V a l l e y   o f   H i n n o m

Ein Rogel

Key

•••• The Jebusite and David's city
——— The Solomonic expansion
–·–·– 8th–7th cent. B.C.E. expansion
- - - - Water systems

 Finds of Biblical period outside the contemporary city

0   100   200
                         m

5
A Spring Called Gihon

NOT ALL OF OLD JERUSALEM'S magic lies within her ancient ramparts. You will discover it in the high and the low places round about, sometimes even by chance. For the city wears her antiquity with a disconcerting carelessness, as if she were quite indifferent to attention. And the past, indeed, is so much everywhere that it is even possible, perhaps, to become a little complacent over it.

Somewhere at the back of your mind, too, you know that significant as much of it may be, it was not the beginning of everything. You sense that before the Wailing Wall, the Crusades, the ramparts of Suleiman the Magnificent, Hadrian and Titus, the Medes and the Persians and the Babylonians, even before the temple and the city itself, there must have been something else. Something that started Jerusalem off.

There was. And if you go deep into the Kidron Valley — the Valley of Jehoshaphat — with some idea of what you are looking for, you will find it. For before everything that is and has been Jerusalem, there was a spring called Gihon, which means "gushing." It lies in a cave at the foot of the eastern slope of the ridge or hill known as Ophel, as lively, it would seem, as when David first saw it 3,000 years ago.

The sight must have pleased this warrior-king, for he had just marched his army from Hebron, and the spring was the only source of fresh water in the area. That is why the Jebusites, whom he had come to dislodge, had built their city on the hill immediately above, rather than on, the adjoining and higher western ridge of the rocky plateau. And that is why David, after he had taken the Canaanite stronghold, made it his new capital. An assured water supply was more precious than fine gold in this part of the world.

The Israelites had arrived at the spring of Gihon with no false hopes. For centuries the Jebusites had resisted attacks on their fortress, although it had fallen once, temporarily, into the hands of Judah. Its impregnability had bred an arrogance so that the new foe was told that only the blind and the lame were needed to repulse them. But this time the taunt miscarried. In the grand strategy of things, the day had dawned when ownership of this ancient citadel was to change hands. And it did so, ironically enough, because of something that down the years had been the Jebusites' greatest asset — their trusted spring.

The vital water supply actually lay outside the city walls, and to reach it the Jebusites had sunk a shaft from within their fortress and then tunneled to the source. To have enclosed the spring within the lower wall would merely have presented the enemy with an easy target from the opposite side of the valley. Instead, he was faced with fortifications well up the hillside, and no protective cover. The Jebusites, in fact, had every reason to feel secure.

But that day they waited in vain for any frontal attack. They were at last to lose their kingdom, through the element of surprise, and with that economy of words in which the Bible has no peer, it tells how this took place. "And David said on that day, 'Whoever would smite the Jebusites, let him get up the water shaft [KJV: gutter] to attack the lame and the blind . . . and whoever shall smite them first shall be chief and commander' . . . and Joab, the son of Zeruiah, went up first, so he became chief" (2 Sam. 5:8 RSV). The site that fell into the hands of David and his men that day was less than eleven acres in extent, but on it began the city that thenceforth was to shape a people's destiny. It was the year 1048 B.C., and since that time the coming of nations against the stronghold of Zion, the City of David, has never ceased.

It was here that David, the former shepherd boy, ruled over a united Judah and Israel for the next thirty-three years, here that he brought the ark of the Lord, here that he looked from his palace upon the beauty of Bathsheba, and here that he died. But before he "went the way of all the earth," David chose the spring of Gihon for another very special purpose. It was to this spot that he directed Zadok the priest and Nathan the prophet to take his son Solomon, mounted on the "royal" mule, and there anoint him king. The Bible narrative gives a picture of a splendid occasion when the trumpet blew, "and the people piped with pipes and rejoiced with great joy so that the earth rent with the sound of them," and all said, "God save king Solomon" (1 Kings 1:39,40).

All, that is, except those who were shouting, "God save king Adonijah" at another celebration a little farther down the Kidron Valley. For the son of David by Haggith had elevated himself lord of the realm without permission, and only the sounds coming from Gihon caused him to stop in the middle of his festivities. On learning the reason for the noise, Adonijah was afraid, and "all the guests [one of whom was Joab of earlier fame] that were with Adonijah rose up, and went every man his own way. . . . Then Solomon sat upon the throne of David his father; and his kingdom was established greatly" (1 Kings 1:49; 2:12).

Was it because of his first adventure at the spring of Gihon that David chose to remember it almost with his dying breath? It does no harm to think so. Today the spring is sometimes called the Fountain of the Virgin because Mary is believed to have washed the clothes of Jesus there, but here again we are in the realm of conjecture.

Strange as it may seem, it is incredibly easy to walk past this historic spot without noticing it. For about it today are the fences of a school playground, and almost over it a double-storied dwelling. These harmonize well with the Arab village of Silwan that sprawls up the opposite hillside, but not with the pillar of Absalom and the tomb of Zechariah farther up toward the Jericho Road. At the bottom of a first flight of steps, and barring the entrance to a large cave, is a semicircular iron grid with a gateway on the right-hand side. Beyond that is another series of steps with a handrail leading down to a smaller and darker opening in the rock, from where, faintly, there comes the sound of moving water.

It is not easy to believe that it was to this somewhat gloomy place the Jerusalems of old owed their existence, that here the wise and mighty Solomon was proclaimed king, and that here, too, began one of the greatest engineering feats of the ancient world. There is no memorial of any kind to mark this historic site.

There is only the spring itself.

You see it from the top of the second lot of steps, a pool of dark, cold-looking water swirling around in its cavern of faintly glistening rock. For a while the sight mesmerizes. Then, on descending farther, something else comes into view — a tunnel leading out from the back of the pool and along which the water is slowly flowing. Whether by

chance or design, you have seen not only the spring of Gihon, but
the beginning of perhaps the most extraordinary aqueduct ever
constructed. It is known as Hezekiah's Tunnel.

The Siloam Pool, the lower end of Hezekiah's Tunnel from the Gihon Spring.

6
Hezekiah's Tunnel

Hezekiah's Tunnel, built to foil Sennacherib's destruction of Jerusalem, extended from the Gihon Spring outside the walls to the Siloam Pool inside the city.

IT IS NOT EVERY DAY that you can stretch out a hand and touch an adamantine rock face in which men sank their picks 2,675 years ago, or traverse a 1,750-foot tunnel dug by those same implements. The experience is one to be remembered, even if it can never be adequately described. It is one thing to walk along the top of Jerusalem's crenelated walls; it is another to walk virtually beneath them through a narrow, winding subterranean aqueduct.

The first may cost you nothing, the latter the price of a guide, a few candles or a torch, and some very old clothes. The former will bring you into contact with the handiwork of Suleiman the Magnificent, a beautifier of Jerusalem in the sixteenth century A.D.; the latter will acquaint you with the handiwork of King Hezekiah, who reigned over the kingdom of Judah from 728 to 699 B.C. The two are worlds and centuries apart, but both testify to Jerusalem's power to survive.

For some 250 years after the anointing of Solomon the spring of Gihon fades from the pages of Scripture. At his death in 970 B.C. David handed over to his son an empire at the zenith of its power, and its glory continued for another forty years. But while Solomon "exceeded all the kings of the earth for riches and for wisdom," his old age was marred by that which was "evil in the sight of the Lord."

Ignoring the plainest of warnings, he built high places for the worship of false gods and goddesses to satisfy his heathen wives, acts that initiated the sundering of the empire but which, because of the worthiness of his father, he was not forced to witness. With Solomon, however, an era ended that was never to return. Because they had forsaken the God who had brought them out of the land of

47

Egypt, a people were to be divided and dispersed. There was to be a sundering that would leave Judah with but one tribe, Benjamin, and the remaining ten in the northern kingdom of Israel. Plunderers from pagan lands were to take their spoil and humiliate a once-proud nation, only the righteousness of some of her prophets and rulers delaying the judgment on Jerusalem.

When Hezekiah came to the throne of Judah at the age of twenty-five, the Assyrians were busy putting an end to the northern kingdom, Shalmanser and Sargon II carrying on the work of destruction and deportation begun by Tiglath-pileser. In 722 B.C. Samaria capitulated after holding off the invaders for three years, and it was not long before the dark shadow of Sennacherib fell across the hills of Judah. After making himself master of forty-seven cities, including Lachish, "the great king of Assyria" turned his attention to Jerusalem, having, as he boasted, imprisoned Hezekiah there "like a bird in a cage."

To meet Sennacherib's demands of tribute, Hezekiah had even to appropriate the treasure of the temple, but this merely gave the city temporary relief. Pressure on its inhabitants increased in the form of subtle propaganda that stressed the futility of resistance and the dangers into which they were being led. "Whereon do ye trust, that ye abide in the siege of Jerusalem?" asked the Assyrian envoys of those gathered on its walls. "Doth not Hezekiah persuade you to give over yourselves to die by famine and by thirst, saying the Lord our God shall deliver us out of the hand of the king of Assyria?" (2 Chron. 32:10,11).

The threat of thirst and starvation was a real one, but it did not hold the terror on this occasion that it might have held. Hezekiah was both a wise and a practical king and, anticipating the siege, he had taken precautions. But the Assyrians' greatest mistake was that "they spoke against the God of Jerusalem . . . and for this cause Hezekiah the king, and the prophet Isaiah the son of Amoz, prayed and cried to heaven" (2 Chron. 32:19,20). In doing so, Hezekiah was not acting out of character. His reign had been one of revival and reformation following the evil and disastrous rule of his father Ahaz. He destroyed the idolatrous altars, cleansed and reopened the temple, and invited all, from Beersheba to Dan, to come to the greatest Passover since Solomon in Jerusalem. For fourteen years the city had prospered.

In the center of the storm about to break over Jerusalem, therefore, two men did not despair. Isaiah had already been permitted a glimpse into the future, and Hezekiah, clothed in sackcloth, had gone to the temple to spread out before the Lord the letter that Sennacherib had sent "to reproach the living God" (2 Kings 19:14,16) — and to pray for deliverance.

Deliverance came with a swiftness that must have astonished even those anticipating it, for that night 185,000 Assyrians were slain in their camp; their king returned "with shame of face" to Nineveh, where he died at the hands of his sons while worshiping in the house of his god Nisroch; and Jerusalem, rejoicing in her good fortune, began what was to be her last century of independence before the Babylonians came and rendered her desolate.

"Behold I will send a blast upon him . . . " (2 Kings 19:7) was how Isaiah had reported the revelation given him of the pending destruction of the Assyrian army, and many accounts support the most sudden mass execution ever to take place. (One hundred thousand perished in the atomic explosion over Hiroshima on August 6, 1945.) Those encamped outside the walls of Jerusalem sometime in the year 701, were not, it would seem, burned, but died from a sudden draught of deadly gas.

It is not likely that Sennacherib or his army ever saw the Gihon spring. Because King Hezekiah, with more foresight than the Jebusites, had taken the precaution of sealing up all the fountains "that ran through the midst of the land, saying, Why should the kings of Assyria come, and find much water?" (2 Chron. 32:4). But he had gone further to minimize the horrors of a siege: he had "stopped the upper watercourse of Gihon and brought it straight down to the west side of the city" (2 Chron. 32:30). That is, he diverted the flow of the spring, still outside the walls, from its normal course down the Kidron Valley, to the Pool of Siloam, inside the city.

What David once made use of to capture Jerusalem from the Jebusites, Hezekiah now used to prevent its surrender to the Assyrians. He extended the tunnel dug by the Jebusites to their vertical shaft by another seventy yards so that water flowed to the reservoir with an overall drop of some twenty-five yards. The average height of this remarkable conduit today is just over six feet, but in 1838 the great explorer of Palestine, Edward Robinson, had to crawl his way through, as did Captain Charles Warren who surveyed Jerusalem for the Palestine Exploration Fund, thirty years later. Some parts of the tunnel were then only two feet high.

Hezekiah set his pick wielders to work at both ends of the aqueduct, and they made their way towards one another with surprising accuracy. What has been described as "the most precious of all ancient Hebrew inscriptions" records the moment of contact:

> . . . and while there was still three cubits [a cubit = eighteen inches] to be cut through, there was heard the voice of a man calling to his fellow, for there was an overlap (or split) in the rock on the right (and on the left). And when the tunnel was driven through, the diggers hewed the rock each man towards his fellow, pick-axe against pick-axe; and the water flowed from the spring toward the reservoir for 1,200 cubits: and the height of the rock above the head of the diggers was a 100 cubits.

The inscription on a panel in the rock face about twenty feet inside the Siloam end of the tunnel was only discovered by chance in 1880. Before it could be removed for safekeeping, it was damaged and stolen by vandals, but it was later recovered in about seven pieces. The Turks, then in control of Jerusalem, sent it to the Istanbul Museum, where it is still. There is a plaster copy of the historic inscription in the Israeli Museum in Jerusalem.

Whether the tunnel that Hezekiah built to foil the evil intentions of Sennacherib was actually of service during the Assyrian threat we shall never know. There were mightier forces acting on behalf of Judah on that occasion. Today the spring of Gihon still wells up in the pool where the tunnel begins. For some dozen paces the icy water will reach almost up to your armpits before you start negotiating the ancient conduit itself. And as the flickering candle lights up the black, damp walls, you may remember perhaps a little of their history.

You may remember why a far-sighted king had this strategic watercourse dug; even that "he was once sick unto death" and that he was told by the prophet Isaiah to set his house in order, for he would die, but that he "wept sore" and called upon the Lord to remember that he had walked before him in truth and with a perfect heart and had done that which was good in his sight (2 Kings 20:3).

But then again you may pass the spring of Gihon by and never see the ancient aqueduct, and that would be a great pity. For you would have missed the opportunity of getting closer to Old Testament history than perhaps anywhere else in Jerusalem.

7
The Threshing-Floor of Araunah

The interior of the Dome of the Rock with the threshing floor that David bought from Araunah, the Jebusite. From this strange slab of unhewn stone sprang Solomon's temple, for this bare rock was to lie almost immediately before the holy chambers in the courtyard of the priests.

WHILE THERE IS NEVER any great certainty that you will set eyes on the Gihon spring or the Siloam tunnel, it is virtually impossible to leave Jerusalem without having stood transfixed for a time before a portion of grayish black rock. It measures some sixty feet by fifty feet, slopes slightly, and, except for a few marks of chiseling, is still in its unhewn, primitive state. You could see something similar to it, no doubt, on any rocky outcrop.

But it would not be quite the same. It would not, for a start, be the summit of Mount Moriah. Nor would it be the center of Islam's second most sacred shrine, as this curious monument is. It wouldn't be the strange slab of rock that was sacred to the Jews centuries before Muhammad is said to have ascended to heaven from it on his winged horse; for that rock is even more inseparable from the history of Jerusalem than the fountain far below in the Valley of the Kidron. But unlike the Gihon spring, this feature of the Judean landscape can hardly be by-passed, for over it rises the famous Dome of the Rock.

And as one stares at this inanimate object thrusting its way up through the floor of the glittering man-made sanctuary, it is as if a world of fantasy has suddenly opened up before one's eyes. The combination of this mass of crude, bare rock and the intricate beauty surrounding it seem to leave no room for reality. All is but an artist's bizarre conception designed to intrigue and excite the senses, and to expect to find some clue to the beginning of things here as one did in the Kidron Valley is to labor under a delusion. These are simply the precincts of a Muslim mosque with an unusual motif and manner of ornamentation. So you are led to believe for a time.

53

It is not until you emerge into the open and in the shade, perhaps, of some tall cyprus tress, contemplate the scene about you that the true meaning of it returns. As the relentless rays of a June sun turn the gold of the immense dome into a blinding white, you remember that this mosque, rearing itself from a paved platform, and unique in the history of architecture because of the cupola with its circle within a double octagon, now occupies the spot where Abraham made an altar upon which to sacrifice his son Isaac. You remember that before the Wailing Wall, before the tunnel of Hezekiah, before David's capture of the ancient stronghold, there was the threshing floor of Araunah, the Jebusite. The rock in the middle of the Muslim shrine was not simply an eccentric accessory to a work of art. It was the rocky prominence from which the chaff of the wheat was blown away 3,000 years ago and more. *It was as important in the genesis of a city as the spring in the valley beneath it.*

It was perhaps even more important. For the history of Jerusalem is in a large measure the history of its temples, and it was from this mass of unhewn stone that they sprang in varying splendor down the centuries. Here was their nucleus, their ready-made altar of burnt offering, which was to lie always immediately before the holy chambers in the courtyard of the priests. Here, some 1,000 years after Abraham, came a penitent David to sacrifice and make one of the most significant purchases in the history of his people.

As fresh storm clouds gather ominously on her horizons today, the mind reels at the number and nature of Jerusalem's decimations. And the enigmatical character of the city is only heightened by the fact that her earliest threat of destruction came from God Himself. After David's exploitation of the Gihon spring to take the Jebusite stronghold, he spent the greater part of the next thirty-three years in waging war, particularly against the Syrians and "the hosts of the Philistines." Israel prospered to the extent that its king was able to ask, "What nation in the earth is like it?" Then one day David decided to take a census, something abhorrent to a nomadic people and which incurred divine displeasure. "Go, number Israel from Beersheba, even to Dan" (1 Chron. 21:2), he had told Joab. For his sin he was given the choice of one of three punishments — seven years of famine, flight before his enemies for three months, or ravaging of the land by a pestilence for three days. He chose the last, and 70,000 people perished.

This shedding of innocent blood was hard to bear. But then David saw an even more frightening thing — an angel with a sword held out over Jerusalem to destroy it. Clothed in sackcloth, he fell upon his face. And perhaps, because of days he still remembered when as a shepherd boy he roamed the hills, he prayed, "Is it not I that commanded the people to be numbered? I it is that have sinned and done evil indeed; but as for these sheep, what have they done? Let thine hand, O Lord my God, be on me, and on my father's house; but not on thy people, that they should be plagued" (1 Chron. 21:17).

That was the day that Jerusalem, after only about thirty years as the center of Hebrew life, survived its first crisis. The angel's avenging hand was stayed and David was told to go up and "rear an altar unto the Lord in the threshing floor of Araunah the Jebusite" (2 Sam. 24:18) — the place where the angel had stood. How significant a command this was only the years would tell, and none could have pleased a thankful David more.

For he loved Jerusalem. This was the city he had made his capital, after God had taken him "from the sheepcote" to be ruler over his people Israel" (1 Chron. 17:7), in which he had looked down from his palace upon the beauty of Bathsheba, the city to which he had brought the ark of the covenant that for 500 years had never had a permanent resting place; where too, he had uttered that cry of anguish: "O my son Absalom . . . , would God I had died for thee!" (2 Sam. 18:33), where he wrote some of the most glorious songs of praise and supplication ever penned and laid bare his grief and repentance in words unparalleled in literature.

And now humbled, Israel's greatest king climbed up from the city he had established on the ridge above the Gihon spring towards the loftier Mount Moriah where he found Araunah threshing wheat on the windy summit. No meeting could have been friendlier, no business transacted in a more amicable fashion. Though offered what he sought for nothing, David insisted on making full payment and bought the actual threshing floor and oxen for fifty shekels of silver and the whole estate of the Jebusite dignitary (perhaps a king) for six hundred shekels of gold. "So the Lord was intreated for the land, and the plague was stayed from Israel" (2 Sam. 24:25).

The purchase was indeed a historic one. To David in his old age had fallen the honor of acquiring the site that was from then on to rank supreme in a nation's history. On the pinnacle of the temple that would be there one thousand years later the Lord of heaven would be tempted by Satan. Around it men would die by thousands and strangers would take possession of it. And as the sun continues to beat down on this "high place" and on those removing their shoes before entering the shrine of gleaming marble and mosaics, the ghosts of the past rise up before you.

Over the threshing floor of Araunah there still stands a temple, but it is not the temple of the people who first built one there. For 1,900 years they have had no sanctuary on this spot. There have been many changes at the place where an angel once stood with a sword drawn over a city. And like the drama of Jerusalem itself, the drama of the site that began when "a man after God's own heart" purchased a bare slab of rock is not yet finished. For how long, one wonders, will the winds of change that have been blowing so vigorously through the rest of Israel leave undisturbed the summit of Mount Moriah.

8
Solomon's Temple

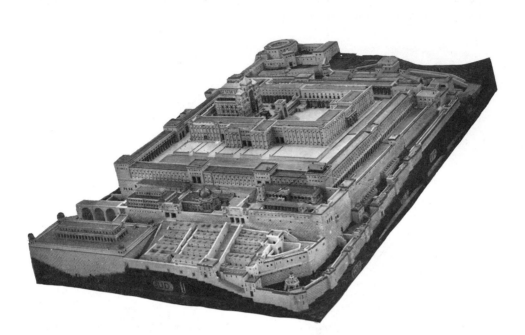

Schick's model of the first temple (1896). Unfortunately, he apparently confused some features with those of Herod's temple.

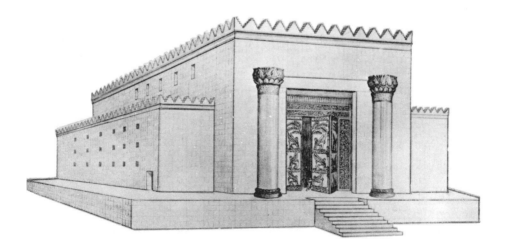

Stevens-Wright replica of the sacred structure (1955).

Solomon replaced the tabernacle of the desert wanderings, with its acacia wood and rams' skins dyed red, with a temple of stone. This was the building that consolidated Jerusalem's religious significance and immortalized his name.

OLD JERUSALEM straddles a triad of hills, its two and a half miles of walls enclosing an area, very nearly square, of some 175 acres. Of these, 35 comprise the present temple site, or, as the Arabs call it today, the Haram es-Sharif, the Noble Sanctuary, a tract of earth that for sheer historic significance, nothing can possibly match. It lies up against the east wall of the city, wrapped in its own deep silence, and with not a little of the uncanny about its empty spaces. The hubbub of the souks is missing here, and even the constant murmur at the Wailing Wall does not penetrate these precincts. It is as if the great flagstones of this paved enclosure were inviting you to hear again the tread of those who have passed this way — the priests and potentates, the men in armor and the men in sackcloth, the lowly and the haughty.

When night falls and a moon, perhaps, turns the great dome to silver, what phantom shapes emerge from the shadows here? Solomon "in all his glory" and surrounded by the splendor of the first temple, and Titus by the blazing inferno of the last; a dazzled Queen of Sheba and a puzzled Pompey; Pilate, Herod and Helena, Chosroes and Omar, Saladin and the Knights Templars, and a host of others, each acting out a different role and serving to add a little to the uniqueness of this stage.

And here also walked the King of Kings. Through the now blocked-up Golden Gate before you in the eastern wall He came that first Palm Sunday; on that high southeast angle known as the pinnacle He resisted the temptation of Satan, and from that northwest corner where once stood the Fortress Antonia He began His last journey on earth. Stand on the parapet of this strangely lonely and

59

desolate sector of the city wall and you can see, almost with a glance, all these places that a Life that changed the world once touched. Olivet, with Gethsemane on its slopes and Bethany beyond, and the Kidron four hundred feet below you on the one side, and the site of the sanctuary where once He raised his voice in anger, on the other — can there be any vantage point on earth to equal this?

And as scenes of long ago unfold before you, instead of the Dome of the Rock in the center of this moonlit enclosure, you see the gleaming walls and pillars of the first Jewish temple, the house that Solomon began to build to the Lord in the fourth year of his reign (1 Kings 6:1). David had died without fulfilling this desire of his heart because "he had shed blood abundantly and had made great wars" (1 Chron. 22:8), but he had prepared the way for Solomon. He had acquired the site of Mount Moriah, the sacred ark was reposing under its tent in the city he had taken from the Jebusites, "hewers and workers of stone and timber, and all manner of cunning men for every manner of work," were ready to start, "of the gold, the silver, and the brass and the iron, there was no number," and "all the princes of Israel" had been commanded to help in the great task (1 Chron. 22:15-17). Almost with his dying breath David had told his son, "Be strong and of good courage, and do it, for the Lord hath chosen thee to build an house for the sanctuary" (1 Chron. 28: 10,20).

This was the sanctuary whose origin lay in another "high place" — the cloud-covered peak of Mount Sinai. Nearly five hundred years previously, similar words had fallen upon the ears of Moses at the end of forty days and forty nights on the mountain. "Speak unto the children of Israel," a voice from a cloud had commanded him, "and let them make me a sanctuary; that I may dwell among them" (Exod. 25:8). This time when Moses came down from Sinai with the second set of tables with the law and all the instructions for the building of the tabernacle, "the skin of his face shone." Until their possession of Jerusalem, Israel was to have a portable shrine throughout all her journeys, covered by the cloud of the Lord in the day and by fire at night. And all "the wise and willing-hearted of Israel" brought gifts for it — goats' hair for the tent; fine twined linen for the curtains; shittim wood for the ark, the altar of burnt-offering, and the table of shewbread; pure gold for the mercy seat; and the menorah or seven-branched candlestick, onyx stones, and oil for the light; and spices for sweet incense — until there was too much.

A year later Moses was able to rear, in the wilderness between the two arms of the Red Sea, the sanctuary built and furnished exactly according to the pattern he had been given.

In a Jerusalem that had been enlarged, Solomon, 480 years later, replaced the tabernacle of the desert wanderings, with its acacia wood and rams' skins dyed red, with a temple of stone. This was the building that consolidated Jerusalem's religious significance and immortalized his name. It was a work upon which the wealth of the nation was lavished, that kept 30,000 people busy for seven years and five months (959–952 B.C.) and during which, legend has it, no laborer died and no tool was ever damaged. Quite near the Damascus Gate there is an entrance today to a vast underground cavern where it is believed the stone was quarried for the temple because "there was neither hammer nor axe nor any tool of iron heard in the house, while it was in building" (1 Kings 6:7). It was paneled with cedar from Lebanon and while the floor of the tabernacle had been the sand of the desert, that of the temple was of gold. Here Solomon laid the sacred ark in the darkness of the Inner Chamber together with the two tablets of stone containing the Ten Commandments. For the Lord who had said "he would dwell in the thick darkness" Solomon had built "an house to dwell in, a settled place . . . to abide in forever" (1 Kings 8:13). And when it was finished, the divine glory filled it as it had the simple tabernacle. In the final act of dedication, 22,000 oxen and 120,000 sheep were sacrificed. Whatever his faults, Solomon did not do things by halves! He built a palace for himself, which took thirteen years, with a great ivory throne overlaid with pure gold. His ships brought gold from Ophir and precious stones and silver, ivory, apes, and peacocks; he had 4,000 stalls for horses brought to him from Egypt and out "of all lands," and he surpassed all the kings of the earth in wisdom and riches.

It was to this temple mount that the Queen of Sheba came with camels of gold and all her retinue, but found herself utterly outshone. After seeing "the ascent by which Solomon went up into the house of the Lord," the apparel of his ministers and cupbearers and the greatness of his wisdom, she graciously conceded that it all exceeded her expectations. And she left Jerusalem with far more than she had brought.

It was here amid the splendor of his throne, his palace, and the first temple, that Solomon reigned for forty years over all Israel before he died and was buried in the city of David his father. He did not know what strange and terrible things were to happen on the crest of a hill that had been the scene of his greatest triumphs. But as you gaze across this fateful strip of earth today, you remember some of them — and wonder.

9
"Give Us a King"

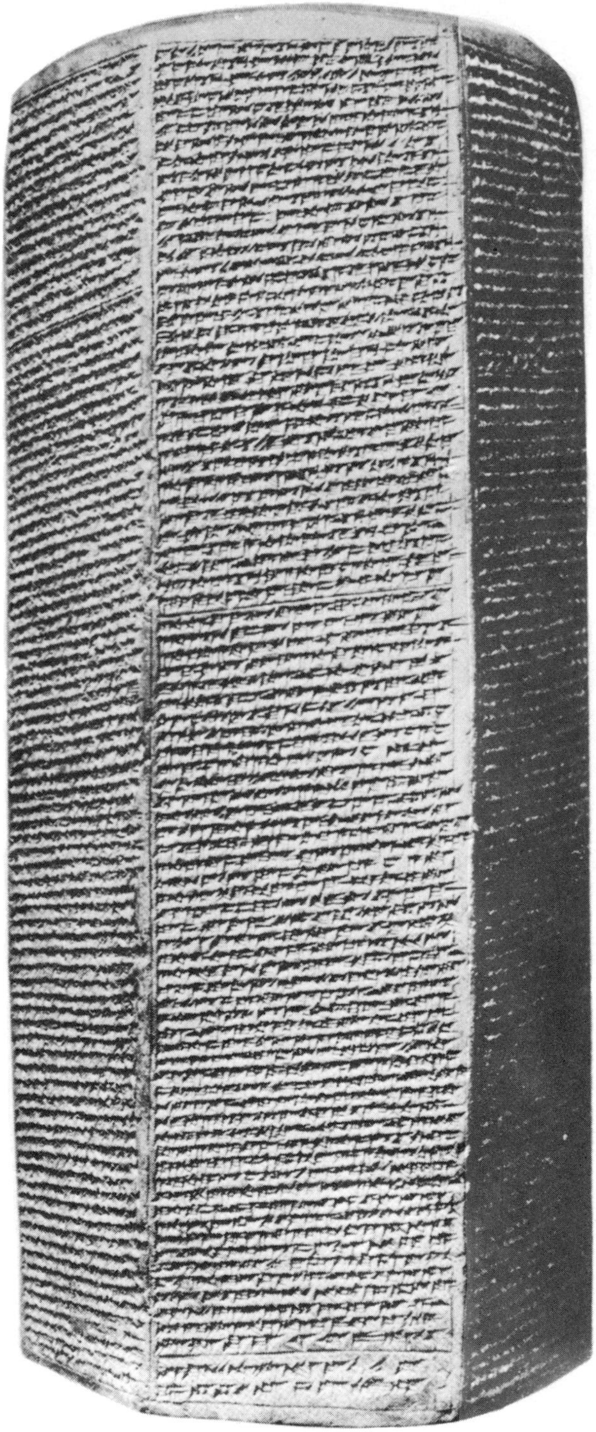

THE TEMPLE THAT **S**OLOMON built lasted for 365 years in a Jerusalem that knew twenty kings and two of her greatest prophets, Isaiah and Jeremiah. But they were years that saw the city and its people move slowly but steadily toward the judgment whose seeds were sown by Solomon himself in his old age. The costly edifices that he had erected were to be desecrated and eventually reduced to ruins and the land about them rendered desolate for seventy years. With the sundering of the unified kingdom, which Saul, David, and Solomon had each ruled for forty years, a new era of failure had dawned.

To the sad and tragic history of her relationship with the God who had brought her out of bondage in Egypt and had preserved her through forty years in the wilderness with miracle upon miracle, Israel was to add another long chapter of ingratitude and apostasy. The pattern of transgression was to be the same as it had been when a murmuring and impatient people paid homage to a molten calf at the foot of Mount Sinai. Though brought safely into the Promised Land, given victory over the idolatrous inhabitants and judges to guide them, they persisted for some three hundred years in bowing down to the gods of the people that were round about. When Samuel, the first of their prophets, "was old and greyheaded," they came to him and cried, "Give us a king . . . that we also may be like all the nations; and that our king may judge us, and go out before us, and fight our battles" (1 Sam. 8:6,20).

The demand was met by solemn warnings from Samuel that a monarchy under the wrong ruler could prove intolerable; it would mean the end of the theocracy, the direct rule of God, that the nation

65

had experienced during the time of the judges. But his protests were in vain, and in the end "the Lord said to Samuel, Harken unto the voice of the people in all that they say unto thee: for they have not rejected thee, but they have rejected me, that I should not reign over them" (1 Sam. 8:7). The die was cast but the disastrous nature of this choice was not fully revealed until the first three kings were in their graves and the kingdom split in two.

The fateful breach came when Jeroboam, a "mighty man of valour" who had rebelled against Solomon and then fled to Egypt, now returned with the idea, no doubt, of putting to the test a prophecy that he would reign over ten tribes. And it was at Shechem, thirty miles north of Jerusalem, where Abram built the first altar to God on entering Canaan, that Rehoboam and Jeroboam came face to face in a confrontation that was to decide the course of events for the next three hundred years.

In exchange for a yoke less grievous than the one they had borne under Solomon, the northern tribes offered their allegiance to Rehoboam. But by one of those strange and imponderable decisions of history, this not unreasonable proposition was rejected. Instead, Rehoboam, acting on the counsel of the "young men that were grown up with him" rather than on that of his older advisers, gave an answer that sent a legitimately angry Israel hurrying "to her tents." "My father made your yoke heavy," he said, "and I will add to your yoke; my father chastised you with whips, but I will chastise you with scorpions" (1 Kings 12:14).

In the circumstances it is not surprising that the person whom Rehoboam, in a further act of folly, sent to collect tribute money from Israel, was stoned to death. When Rehoboam himself fled in his chariot to Jerusalem, the stage was set for two hundred years of intermittent civil war and eventual subjection to the Assyrian and Babylonian empires.

In the north Jeroboam made Shechem his capital and lost no time in setting the pattern of idolatry that was to be followed by every one of the eighteen kings that followed him. To rival the temple on Mount Moriah, he set up two calves of gold and, with a masterly touch of subtle persuasion, told his subjects: "It is too much for you to go up to Jerusalem; behold thy gods, O Israel, which brought thee up out of the land of Egypt" (1 Kings 12:28).

This half of the Hebrew nation plumbed the depths under the reign of Ahab and his wife Jezebel when only the miracle-working

Elisha was able to arrest the spread of Baal worship. The warnings of her prophets, however, fell mostly on deaf ears, and during the siege of Samaria by the Syrians "an ass's head was sold for fourscore pieces of silver" (2 Kings 6:25), and starvation drove the besieged to terrible acts. "They that were brought up in scarlet," Jeremiah was to write many years later, "embrace dunghills" (Lam. 4:5).

This was but the prelude, however, to total disaster, and it was from the hand of the rising power of Assyria that Israel received the final retribution for her wickedness. Between 734 and 721 B.C. her cities were laid waste and her people deported. Samaria finally fell to Sargon II after a siege of three years, and its population was replaced by foreigners.

Judgment on Judah was delayed by some 130 years. When the northern kingdom fell, Jerusalem was under the rule of her thirteenth king, Hezekiah. Seven more were to reign there before she, too, was to "see the heathen enter her sanctuary and spread their hands upon all her pleasant things" (Lam. 1:10). Success smiled on the little southern kingdom during the reign of the three monarchs who succeeded Rehoboam, on one occasion 500,000 chosen men of Israel perishing in battle with her.

But the picture changed drastically with the accession to the throne of Jehoram at the age of thirty-two. He was the son of a good father, but chose the wrong wife, Athaliah, daughter of the infamous Ahab and Jezebel, and began his eight-year reign by putting his brothers to the sword. All his sons except the youngest were carried off by the Philistines and the Arabians, and he himself died of "sore diseases," departing "without being desired" and being buried not in the sepulchres of the kings (2 Chron. 21:19,20). Ahaziah reigned for only a year and when Athaliah heard that he had been slain in Samaria, she destroyed all the royal seed of Judah, except the infant Joash who was hidden in the temple. For the next six years *Athaliah sat on the throne of Judah, the only woman ever to do so.*

No Shakespearean plot unfolds more dramatically than the next events in Jewish history. And it was in the enclosure across which the Dome of the Rock now throws its immense shadow that they reached their climax. In the somewhat eerie stillness it is not difficult to relive the whole tense coronation of the seven-year-old Joash, masterminded by the priest Jehoiada. The Levites came out of all the cities of Judah and gathered around the king. Jehoiada gave to the captains spears, and bucklers, and shields that had been King

David's in the house of the Lord and he placed all the people, "every man having his weapon in his hand, from the right side of the temple to the left . . ." (2 Chron. 23:9,10). Here, perhaps on the spot where one is standing, the boy Joash had the crown placed on his head, and Jehoiada and his sons anointed him and said, "God save the king."

Instead of someone standing in modern dress on the porch of the great Muslim shrine, there was a distraught, tragic-looking figure standing among the people in the house of the Lord. The sound of the trumpets and the praising of the king had brought Athaliah to the temple, and on realizing what was happening, she began to rend her clothes and cried out, "Treason, treason!" (2 Chron. 23:13).

The hour had come when she was about to reap what she had sown, but Jehoiada had given orders that she was not to be put to death in the sanctuary. But after they had seized her and taken her to the "horse gate by the king's house," they slew her. Images that had been set up in Jerusalem were destroyed and the people then set the young king "upon the throne of his kingdom. And all the people of the land rejoiced, and the city was quiet after they had slain Athaliah with the sword" (2 Chron. 23:20,21).

10
The Courageous Jeremiah

A S THE YEARS PASSED, the fortunes of Jerusalem continued to vary with each king that sat on her throne. And always at the center of the vicissitudes was the temple that Solomon had built. It was either being plundered and closed or restored and sanctified. It was Ahaz who, after the long and prosperous reign of Uzziah, and then Jotham, "shut up the doors of the house of the Lord, cut its vessels in pieces, and made altars in every corner of Jerusalem"; he reintroduced Baal worship, "burnt his children in the fire" and made sacrifices "on the hills, and under every green tree" (2 Chron. 28:3,24).

With the treasures of the temple he bought the help of the Assyrian king Tiglath-pileser when Jerusalem was threatened by Syria and Israel from the north, by the Edomites from the east, and by the Philistines from the west. In one day King Pekah of Israel slew 120,000 of the army of Judah, "all valiant men," and took captive to Samaria 200,000 men, women, and children. Under Ahaz, Judah was brought to a point in her moral and spiritual decay where only a revival in depth or a miracle could save her.

She experienced both during the reign of her next king, Hezekiah, whose first acts were the destruction of the images and the restoration of temple worship. His trusted adviser was the great prophet Isaiah. Together they were able to invoke the divine intervention that saved Jerusalem from Sennacherib in 701 B.C. Here amid the somewhat faded splendor of the Solomonic temple stood now the chief of the writing prophets, seeing in his visions far beyond the impending disaster and captivity.

To Isaiah was given the picture of the promised Messiah, the suffering Christ in all His humility, so amazingly accurate that he might have been writing at the foot of the Cross. And the visions that he had "in the days of Uzziah, Jotham, Ahaz, and Hezekiah, kings of Judah," went even further to the time when "violence shall no more be heard in thy land, wasting nor destruction within thy borders; but thou shalt call thy walls Salvation, and thy gates Praise" (Isa. 60:18).

To the Jerusalem of his day Isaiah brought a vision of God's plan for the redemption of man. He saw God's mercy and His majesty, and just as clearly the day of His wrath, that in the divine reckoning "there is no peace . . . to the wicked" (Isa. 57:21). His ministry brought deliverance to the city, but the dark shadow that Sennacherib had cast across it was one day to return, and this time there would be no escape.

The good that Hezekiah had done in the twenty-nine years he sat on the throne of Judah was soon erased by his son. Manasseh's reign of fifty-five years was the longest and the worst in the history of the southern kingdom. He lost no time in reestablishing Baal worship and setting up an idol in the temple. He indulged in sorcery and served the hosts of heaven — sun, moon, stars, and planets. In the days of a people's worst idolatry an image of Moloch was erected in the Valley of Hinnom below Jerusalem's southwest wall, where refuse from the city was burnt. Here human sacrifices were offered, and here Manasseh sacrificed children in the fire. Whatever chance the Hebrews may have had of surviving as an independent nation now vanished completely, and not even the subsequent reformation under Josiah was able to prevent their Babylonian exile.

The precincts of the first temple that were now to echo with the vain pleadings and warnings of Jeremiah would soon be filled with the noise of Nebuchadnezzar's armies. No wonder the last of Judah's prophets before the exile presents a lonely, tragic figure as he stands "in the court of the Lord's house" (Jer. 19:14) and delivers his prophecies of certain destruction. The sensitive Jeremiah had great cause to weep. Isaiah saw Jerusalem delivered from the hand of the enemy; Jeremiah was to see the city in its death throes.

Jeremiah had the unenviable task of telling a city that had become worse than Sodom that "it shall be given into the hand of the king of Babylon, and he shall burn it with fire" (Jer. 21:10). He had to plead for repentance, knowing that it was too late for repentance. He gave utterance to some of the saddest words of the Bible when he was forced to cry, "The harvest is past, the summer is ended, and we are not saved" (Jer. 8:20). Stand in the gate of the temple, he was told, and say, "Cut off thine hair, O Jerusalem, and cast it away. . . . I will cause to cease . . . from the streets of Jerusalem the voice of mirth, and the voice of gladness . . . the land shall be desolate, and I will cast you out of my sight. . . . This is a nation that obeyed not the voice of their God" (Jer. 7:15,28,29,34).

It is not all that surprising perhaps that King Jehoiakim burned the roll prepared by Jeremiah and the scribe Baruch in which the fate of Jerusalem and its people were vividly recorded, and the reason for the judgment clearly set out. Nor that the inconsolable prophet was later accused of treason and imprisoned. His message was not a popular one. But he preached it faithfully for forty-two years in the face of immense opposition, ridicule, and persecution. He began his ministry in the thirteenth year of Josiah, about 626 B.C., and was "in the court of the prison" (Jer. 38:28) in 586 B.C. when Jerusalem was taken.

They were the years in which a new Babylonian empire spread out from the south Euphrates valley, broke the power of Assyria in 607 B.C., and crushed Egypt two years later. It was Jeremiah who saw the armies of Nebuchadnezzar reduce Jerusalem's population and buildings in three separate incursions over a period of twenty years. He saw its kings, its princes, its royal seed, all its mighty men of valor, craftsmen, and smiths, all that were "strong for war," carried off to Babylon. None remained except the poorest sort of people of the land. Also to the Chaldean capital went the treasure and the vessels of gold from the temple.

For a year and a half the city held out under its last king, Zedekiah, before the final curtain descended on this era of Jewish history. It fell in the sacred precincts where Jeremiah had implored the nation to turn and serve the living God. Here "in the house of their sanctuary" were slain the young and "him that stooped for age" (2 Chron. 36:17). Toward none did the enemy show any compassion. Where the Assyrians had failed, the Chaldeans succeeded. They "burnt the house of God, and brake down the walls of Jerusalem, and burnt all the palaces thereof with fire and . . . them that had escaped from the sword carried he away to Babylon; where they were servants . . . until the reign of the kingdom of Persia" (2 Chron. 36:19),

To the courageous Jeremiah the captors gave a choice of either going into exile or remaining in Jerusalem. He chose the latter, but eventually died in Egypt. Before he left the stricken capital forever, he uttered his last lament over her: "How doth the city sit solitary, that was full of people! How is she become as a widow! she that was great among the nations, and princess among the provinces, how is she become tributary!" (Lam. 1:1). If you listen carefully, you can hear the whole of this lament chanted on Fridays at the Wailing Wall.

And if you watch very carefully as a moon lights up this great paved courtyard of the temple site, you may see, perhaps, the ghosts of Solomon and David, Bathsheba and the Queen of Sheba, the good and the bad kings of Judah, the great Isaiah, the wicked Jezebel and the devilish Athaliah, the mighty Nebuchadnezzar and the faithful, weeping Jeremiah, pass to and fro about the gleaming Muslim shrines.

Clay tablets found in Babylon and dated 595 and 570 B.C., listing rations of oil and barley given to prisoners. Jehoiachin and his sons are included.

11
Return From Babylon

The Cyrus Cylinder, which gives an account of the Persian's capture of Babylon in 539 B.C. and sanctions the return of Israel to her own land.

FOR THE NEXT FIFTY YEARS (586–536 B.C.) Jerusalem is lost to sight. She knows only the obscurity and desolation predicted for her by prophet after prophet. The seemingly impossible has happened, "the adversary and the enemy have entered into her gates." From the City of God the people have gone to the city of Nebuchadnezzar; from a city of a single sanctuary to a city of over 50 temples and 1,300 altars to strange gods. Because they had persisted in idol worship "until there was no remedy" (2 Chron. 36:16), they were taken captive to the metropolis of pagan rites and superstitions. But it was in Babylon with its great temple to Marduk, its luxury and its licentiousness, that the Jews were finally cured of idolatry.

There must have been something particularly bitter about this captivity, for it was endured within 140 miles of where 1,500 years before Abraham had set out under divine decree for the Promised Land. And what was there to show for all those years? Only a road, it seemed, that led backwards, signposted with failure after failure. When Terah and his family left the flourishing port of Ur at the confluence of the Tigris and Euphrates rivers, it was to find a land where a nation could be established free of idolatry. Behind them was a city that worshiped the moon-god Sin and his consort Nin, or Ishtar, whose shrines crowned a dominating ziggurat of solid burnt brick. On their way westward they would have passed close to another city whose star was rising under king Hammarubi and where terraced towers and temples to Marduk, supreme among the gods, were piercing the sky. This was the Babylon that was to color the history of empires, whose splendor would dazzle the ancient world, but whose chief characteristic would always be idolatry.

And it was to the most magnificent Babylon of them all that the descendants of Abraham had now come. They were back where idolatry had its genesis after the Flood; where that "mighty one in the earth" (Gen. 10:8), Nimrod, grandson of Ham and later deified as the god Marduk, built the first great ziggurat. "And the beginning of his kingdom," we are told, "was Babel" (Gen. 10:10). But the Babylon of Nimrod passed, as did the one belonging to the first "golden age" under Hammarubi. The Hittites reduced the city to ashes, and the Assyrians destroyed it three times. It was Sennacherib who leveled it in 689 B.C., just twelve years after the supernatural destruction of his own army at Jerusalem, and who brought its treasures back to a Nineveh that "gleamed like the sun" on the Tigris. Then Assurbanipal dealt the restored city a blow that it was thought had finally settled its fate. But it was not Babylon, but the Assyrian capital of Nineveh that was to disappear from history first.

To a reluctant Jonah, it may be remembered, came the commission about the year 850 B.C., to go to Nineveh "that great city and cry against its wickedness" (Jonah 1:2). The charge was not obeyed the first time but after his experience with the great fish, the prophet fulfilled his task, declaring "yet forty days and Nineveh shall be overthrown." But much to Jonah's surprise, it would seem, the people of Nineveh "believed God . . . and put on sackcloth, from the greatest unto the least of them," and even the king "sat in ashes" (Jonah 3:5,6). This gesture of repentance gained the city nearly two hundred years' respite during which time it was permitted to put an end to the northern kingdom of Israel. But the city that the prophets likened to a den of ravaging lions, feeding on the blood of nations, the rejoicing city that "dwelt carelessly," that said in her heart: "I am, and none else beside me" (Isa. 4:7,8), reaped at last the whirlwind that her Assyrian rulers had sown.

Her destroyer was Nabopolasser, viceroy of Babylon who joined forces with the Medes, and after a two-year siege rendered Nineveh, in 612 B.C., "empty, void, and waste." With the chariots raging in the streets and jostling one against another in the broad ways (Nahum 2:4), the last king of Nineveh set fire to his palace and perished there with all his treasures. The desert sands closed over the "city of lies and robbery" and for the next 2,500 years even the place where the once-proud metropolis had stood was forgotten. Today, near the ancient site, the oil wells of Mosul, Iraq's second largest city, yield up their precious "liquid gold."

With Nineveh but a memory, at the center of a new Chaldean empire rose another Babylon, more majestic than any before. What Nabopolasser had begun, his son Nebuchadnezzar completed, and it was to a city at the height of its splendor that the Jews of a stricken Jerusalem had come. To a city whose "hanging gardens" were one of the seven wonders of the ancient world, whose magnificent temples to pagan gods were everywhere to be seen, and where Daniel had already been living for twenty years. It was here by the rivers of Babylon that Judah wept when she remembered Zion, where she hung her harps on the willows and asked how she could sing the Lord's song in a strange land.

But she did just that for another fifty years — until the night Belshazzar gave a feast to a "thousand of his lords" and as they were drinking from the vessels taken from the temple in Jerusalem a hand suddenly began writing on the wall of the palace. It was Daniel, the interpreter of dreams, who informed the king that he had been weighed in the balance and had been found wanting and that God had divided his kingdom and given it to the Medes and Persians. No wonder Belshazzar's countenance changed and his knees "smote one against another" (Dan. 5:6). By diverting the Euphrates into a new channel, the forces of Cyrus took Babylon by surprise, and that night, in the year 539 B.C., the king of the Chaldeans was slain (Dan. 5:30).

Babylon continued to flourish as part of the Persian Empire for another two hundred years, but its sun began to set with the shift of world power from Asia to the Mediterranean. It was here that Alexander the Great came after his conquest of India: and it was here that he died six months later, on 13 June, 323 B.C., at the age of thirty-two, while in the midst of immense plans for the future. The end of the city was now in sight and its fate was sealed when Seleucia was founded on the Tigris by one of Alexander's heirs.

The prophecies of Isaiah and Jeremiah centuries before were about to be fulfilled. "And Babylon, the glory of the kingdoms, the beauty of the Chaldees' excellency, shall be as when God overthrew Sodom and Gomorrah. The wild beasts of the desert shall lie there; and their houses shall be full of doleful creatures; and owls shall dwell there" (Isa. 13:21,22). It would "become heaps, a dwellingplace for dragons, an astonishment, and an hissing, without an inhabitant" (Jer. 51:37). Judgment would descend on its graven images, and "as she hath caused the slain of Israel to fall, so at

Babylon shall fall the slain of all the earth. . . . The broad walls of
Babylon shall be utterly broken, and her high gates shall be burned
with fire" (Jer. 51:49,58). All this came to pass, and sixty miles north
of Baghdad the railway line passes today within a few yards of ruins
of what once was the most splendid city on earth.

But while the sands of the desert closed over Nineveh and later
over Babylon, a new day had dawned for the city that conquerors
imagined they had crushed forever. To Jerusalem had returned a
remnant of the nation that had gone into captivity for seventy years.
"Go and build the house of the Lord God of Israel," Cyrus, king of
Persia, had told the exiles in Babylon soon after he had assumed
control of the city (Ezra 1:2). And nearly 50,000 Jews had taken their
horses and their mules and their camels and 5,400 gold and silver
vessels that Nebuchadnezzar had helped himself to from the temple,
and they made the four-months' journey back to Zion. They were
under the command of a man called Zerubbabel, who would have
been king if there had been a kingdom, for he was the grandson of
King Jehoiachin. Instead, he had been appointed governor of Judah,
and he gave his name to Jerusalem's second temple.

That this temple was to lack the grandeur of Solomon's became
evident at the laying of the foundations when, according to Ezra the
scribe and great reformer of these times, "ancient men who had seen
the first house, wept with a loud voice." But feelings were apparently mixed over the new sanctuary, for it was hard to distinguish
between "the noise of the shout of joy and the noise of the weeping
of the people" (Ezra 3:12,13). Missing, however, from the completed
temple was the sacred ark and the Shekinah glory that had previously shrouded the mercy seat in the Inner Chamber. For the sifting
of the Jewish nation through the nations had begun. Power had now
passed from it to the Gentiles under whose rule Israel was to remain
for the next 2,500 years.

Jerusalem's restoration was a trial of a people's faith and for-
titude. By means of letters of subtle accusation to Babylon concerning "building the rebellious and bad city" (Ezra 4:12), adversaries
round about Jerusalem succeeded in stopping the work on the temple and the walls for fifteen years. But Darius, in 520 B.C., confirmed
the decree of Cyrus and within four years another temple stood
where many years ago a great king of Israel had built a house for his
God.

Here also came Ezra, some sixty years later, with an additional

1,800 exiles laden with silver and gold from the treasury in Babylon. And here he also found a situation that made him rend his garments in despair. For the Jews had taken strange wives from the people of the land, something forbidden them from time immemorial, temple services and sacrifices had been neglected, and immorality was prevalent. It was sufficient to make the priest, steeped in the law of Moses, cry out and say, "O my God, I am ashamed and blush to lift up my face to thee, my God; for our iniquities are increased over our head, and our trespass is grown up into the heavens" (Ezra 9:6).

But through passionate and frank confession of his people's sins, Ezra was able to initiate a swift and remarkable reformation. The temple that he had come to beautify, in whose courts a great congregation pledged obedience to the statutes of their God, was to last for five hundred years — one hundred years longer than its predecessor. It was to last until the days of Herod the Indumean, when a third temple would rise about the threshing floor of Araunah the Jebusite, and a greater than Ezra would worship there and prophesy.

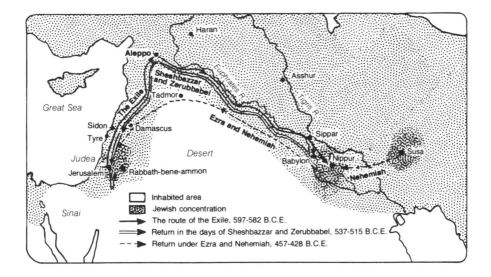

Israel's return from the Babylonian Captivity.

12
Nehemiah the Patriot

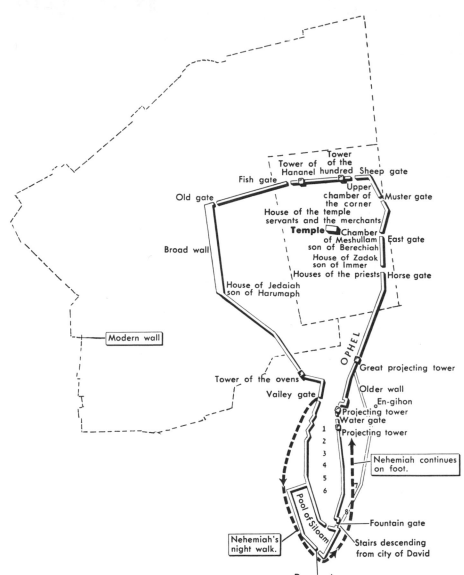

Tower of the hundred
Tower of Hananel
Fish gate
Old gate
Broad wall
Sheep gate
Upper chamber of the corner
Muster gate
House of the temple servants and the merchants
Temple
Chamber of Meshullam son of Berechiah
House of Zadok son of Immer
Houses of the priests
East gate
Horse gate
House of Jedaiah son of Harumaph
Modern wall
OPHEL
Great projecting tower
Tower of the ovens
Valley gate
Older wall
En-gihon
Projecting tower
Water gate
Projecting tower
1
2
3
4
5
6
Nehemiah continues on foot.
8
Pool of Siloam
Fountain gate
Nehemiah's night walk.
Stairs descending from city of David
Dung gate

1   Upper house of the king
2   House of Azariah
3   House of Benjamin and Hasshub
4   House of Eliashib the high priest
5   Ascent to the armory
6   House of the mighty men
7   Artificial pool
8   Sepulchres of David

0   50   100   150 yards
0   50   100 meters

The rebuilding of Jerusalem's walls after the Babylonian Captivity. Nehemiah saw the walls of Jerusalem rebuilt 142 years after their destruction in 586 B.C., one-tenth of the surrounding population brought into the city to live, and the restoration of the temple services.

M AKE YOUR WAY for a while along the sentry walk that tops the walls of present-day Jerusalem and the ghost of Nehemiah must appear at some point on the aged battlements — perhaps with a spear in one hand and a trowel in the other, his eyes still blazing with patriotism. For not these walls, but similar ones rose under Nehemiah's direction in fifty-two days! And with infinite modesty, the one-time "cupbearer" to King Artaxerxes tells us himself how it all happened.

How that in the year 445 B.C. he had learned while at the palace at Shushan (or Susa), the ancient capital of Persia, of the plight of Jerusalem, that his melancholy had been observed by the king and he had explained it thus: "Why should not my countenance be sad, when the city, the place of my fathers' sepulchres, lieth waste, and the gates thereof are consumed with fire?" (Neh. 2:3). This was no less than the truth. It was seventy-one years since the temple had been completed, but Jerusalem still lacked the essential feature of any self-respecting city of the fifth century. It was a city without walls, without proper fortifications. It was "large and great, but the people were few therein, and the houses were not builded" (Neh. 7:4).

Nehemiah, the bold patriot, by his faith and his courage, changed all that. He left the court of Artaxerxes with letters of authority and a royal escort, but he encountered opposition of every nature before his task was accomplished. It was at night that he was forced, with only a few chosen men, to make his preliminary survey of the "walls that were broken down." When it was seen that he was determined Jerusalem should no longer "be a reproach," the enemy

tried ridicule. "What do these feeble Jews? Will they fortify themselves? . . . Will they revive the stones out of the heaps of the rubbish
which are burned? . . . Even that which they build, if a fox go up, he
shall even break down their stone wall" (Neh. 4:2,3).

Nehemiah prayed and got on with the job, "for the people had a
mind to work." Then the hostile neighbors tried a show of force
backed by repeated threats of open war. This was answered by more
prayer and the setting of a watch day and night, so rigorous, it
seems, that no one ever put off his clothes except for washing! It also
compelled Nehemiah to divide his forces, half holding "the spears
from the rising of the morning till the stars appeared," and the other
half building, everyone with his sword girded by his side. "And he
that sounded the trumpet was by me" (to summon aid to those who
might be hard pressed at any particular portion of the wall) (Neh.
4:6,18,23).

One might be tempted to believe there was a little embroidery
here on the part of Judah's resolute governor if the picture painted
had not such a striking affinity with one that has colored Israel's
history for the past twenty-five years. There is a parallel of situations
made even more remarkable by the length of time separating them
that intrigues and fascinates. Like those wall builders of old, the
modern Israeli has had to work virtually with sword in one hand and
trowel in the other to secure a home of his own.

Nehemiah saw the walls of Jerusalem rebuilt 142 years after their
destruction in 586 B.C., one-tenth of the surrounding population
brought into the city to live, and the restoration of the temple
services. He went, after a time, back to Persia, but paid a second visit
to Jerusalem. Where he died, we do not know, but it does not take
much imagination to suspect he would like to have died in Jerusalem, where the walls he had built later barred the way sometimes
to the armies of the Ptolemies, the Greek kings of Egypt, and sometimes to the armies of the Seleucides, the Greek kings of Syria, and to
whose defense there were to rise new patriots. In the city where
Antiochus Epiphanes wrought havoc, defiled the temple by offering
up a pig on the altar, and where he burnt every copy of the Scriptures
he could lay hands on. In a Jerusalem reconquered by the Maccabees,
in which they established a new Jewish dynasty, and from where
they governed an independent Judea for one hundred years.

But neither the patriotism of Nehemiah, nor of those who followed him, was enough. The last great power that Daniel had seen in

his vision in Babylon was beginning her conquest of the world. Soon Pompey, entangled in the civil strife of the Hasmoneans, would bring the Roman Legions for the first time to the Judean capital. In the city's seventeenth siege since David took it from the Jebusites, he would breach its defenses, slay 12,000 of its inhabitants and then stand stupified in the Inner Chamber of the temple because it held "not a single image of a material god." The year would be 63 B.C. And a young Edomite, called Herod, who was to become king of the Jews, would be ten years old.

Jerusalem would have turned her face to the dawn that her people had been looking for ever since the promise of a Messiah had been given. But she would not recognize the one who would come to her temple, heal the sick in her streets, and speak as no other had spoken. The dawn would turn into a day "of wasteness and desolation of clouds and thick darkness" (Zeph. 1:15). And this time it would not be Nehemiah who would weep over the city, but Jesus of Nazareth.

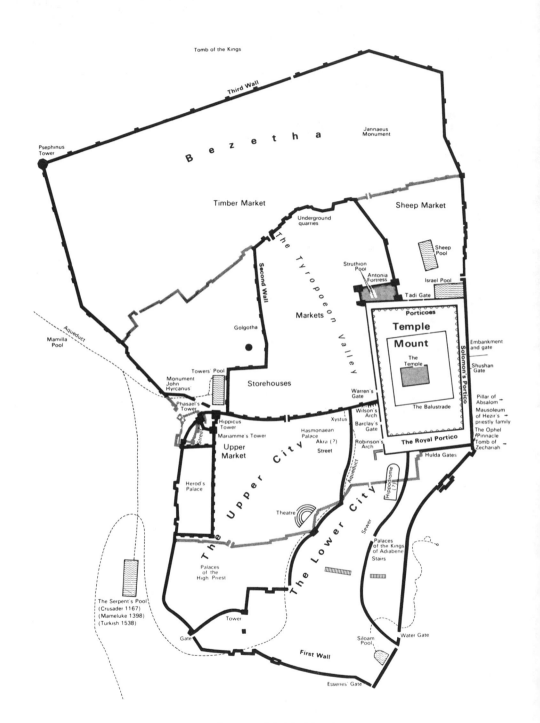

Jerusalem in the Second Temple Period (538-70 B.C.).

PART II
The Darkest Hour

Rejoice greatly, O daughter of Zion; shout, O daughter of Jerusalem: behold, thy King cometh unto thee: he is just, and having salvation; lowly, and riding upon an ass, and upon a colt the foal of an ass.
— Zechariah 9:9

13
The Romans Arrive

Now at this time the Jews held the following
cities of Syria. . .

(Antiquities 13:395)

PHOENICIA

Tyre

Antiochia

Seleucia

Ptolemais

GALILEE

Taricheae

Gamala

Asochis

Arbel

Hippus

Philoteria

Gaulana

Dium

Geba

Sepphoris

Mt. Tabor

Abila

Dora

Gadara

GALAADITIS

Mediterranean Sea

Strato's Tower

Scythopolis

Pella

SAMARIA

Gerasa

Apollonia

Samaria

Ammathus

Shechem

Alexandrium

Joppa

Pegae

Gedor

Philadelphia

Adida

Gazara

JUDEA

Esbus

Jamnia

Azotus

Jerusalem

Hyrcania

Medeba

Ascalon

Hyrcania

Beth-zur

Lemba

Anthedon

Marisa

Macherus

Gaza

Adora

Hebron

Aristobulias

En-gedi

IDUMEA

Masada

MOABITIS

Dead Sea

Eglaim

Raphia

Beer-sheba

Oronaim

Rhinocorura

Elusa

Gabalis

Zoar

NABATEANS

```
0      5      10 miles
0   5  10  15 km
```

.... District border

⊡ Fortress

⌂ Greek city held by Janneus

NOT FAR FROM **B**ETHLEHEM stands a cone-shaped hill that was once "encompassed with circular towers approached by a strait ascent of steps of polished stones, in number two hundred." Within this citadel were royal and very rich apartments, of a structure that provided both for security and for beauty. To it water was brought from a great way off at vast expense, and the plain that was about it "was full of edifices not inferior to any city in largeness."[1]

Here, in 4 B.C. came a great procession headed by a slowly borne bier of solid gold and embroidered with precious stones of great variety. On it, draped in purple, was the body of Herod the Great, a diadem encircling his head and a scepter in his right hand. Following the bier came the guards, then marched "the whole army in the same manner as they used to go out to war, and five hundred domestic servants with sweet spices in their hands." It was a funeral that lacked nothing in outward pomp and pageantry. The body had been carried in state for "two hundred furlongs" from the summer palace in Jericho to the fortress-tomb that Herod had prepared for himself nearly thirty-seven years before.

The Herodium, as it was called, was much less remote than other places of this sort that he had built — Masada, farther south in the heart of the Judean Wilderness, or Machaerus on the barren heights of Moab above the Dead Sea where Salome danced before Herod Antipas and John the Baptist was beheaded. Over seventy years later the Herodium gave refuge for a time to Jewish rebels after

---

[1]The quotations in this chapter are taken from Josephus, *Antiquities of the Jews* and *Wars of the Jews.*

the fall of Jerusalem. Recent excavations have revealed stone cannon balls used as ammunition for catapult machines. But of Herod and his treasures there is no trace.

Less than three miles away from where that spectacular entombment took place, a star had stopped in its course across the heavens only a few months before. For the world a new age had begun whose conflicting forces were to meet with incalculable consequences in a Jerusalem that Herod had first conquered and then adorned with architectural masterpieces.

But it is not with the creation of beauty that history has equated the man whose life bridged, as it were, two eras. We remember Herod, not because he rebuilt the Jewish temple on a scale that surpassed Solomon's, but because he ordered the massacre of the innocents at Bethlehem. He would have destroyed the One who was to inaugurate a new order and issue a new commandment if he could have done so. It was to Jerusalem that wise men from the East had come seeking Him who was born "king of the Jews." And it was here that Herod, when he was seventy years old, planned the crime that was to make his name forever synonymous with cruelty.

He knew well enough that it was not he whom the Magi were looking for. He had not been born with royal blood in his veins; nor was he racially a Jew. He was of Arab stock. His father, Antipater, was an Idumean, the name the Greeks and the Romans used for an Edomite, a descendant of Esau. And it was only because one of the Maccabees had conquered Edom in southern Palestine and forced Judaism on the inhabitants that Herod was able to become king of the Jews.

The way to the throne was paved for him at the start by his father who became the power behind the scenes in the closing years of the Hasmonean dynasty. Civil war was raging between Hyrcanus and Aristobulus when Pompey, flushed with military triumphs for Rome, diverted his attention from trouble at Petra to Jerusalem to try to restore peace.

The vacillating conduct of Aristobulus, whose party finally retreated into the temple fortress, left Pompey with little alternative but to attack this stronghold, once he had managed to fill in the ditch and deep valley on its northern side. He then erected "high towers upon the bank and brought those engines which they had fetched from Tyre near the wall, and tried to batter it down; and the slingers of stones beat off those that stood above them, and drove them away; but the towers on this side of the city made very great resistance, and were indeed extraordinary both for largeness and magnificence."

It was the first of three sieges, according to Josephus, in which advantage was taken by the Romans of the Jewish practice not to join combat with the enemy on the Sabbath. "For though our law gives us leave to defend ourselves against those that begin to assault us, it does not permit us to meddle with our enemies while they do anything else. Which, when the Romans understood, on those days we call Sabbaths they threw nothing at the Jews, nor came to any pitched battle with them, but raised up earthern banks, and brought their engines into such forwardness, that they might do execution the next day."

One can hardly imagine a more galling situation to be in, yet it was two months before the Romans penetrated to where the priests were still offering up sacrifices, "thinking it better to suffer whatever came upon them at their very altars than to omit anything that their laws required of them." Their blood mingled with that of 12,000 others slain that day, some by the Romans and some by other Jews. It was but a foretaste, however, of what was to happen 133 years later. Pompey gazed that day with wonder on what "it was unlawful for any other men to see except the high priests — the golden table of shrewbread, the holy candlestick, and the pouring vessels in the Inner Sanctuary. But he touched none of the two thousand talents of sacred money, and in this point acted in a manner that was worthy of his virtue."

The siege of Jerusalem was over, though there would be another before the dawn of a new era. Pompey ordered the cleansing of the temple, restored the high priesthood to Hyrcanus, declared Jerusalem tributary to the Romans, and confined "the whole nation of Judea which had elevated itself so high before within its own bounds." He then set off for Rome "carrying bound along with him" Aristobulus, his two sons Alexander and Antigonus and two daughters. Antipater, sensing trouble, had sent Herod, a boy of ten, with his mother back to Petra, the Nabataean capital.

Sixteen years passed. The Romans conquered the world and fought one another. Crassus, a member of the First Triumvirate, was slain by the Parthians after he had plundered the temple in Jerusalem. Julius Caesar spent nine years subduing the Gauls and then returned to a jealous Pompey and a hostile Senate. Refusing to disband his army, he crossed the Rubicon on January 10 in the year 49 B.C. and eighteen months later defeated Pompey at Pharsalus in Thessaly. Within another month Pompey lay dead in Egypt, treacherously murdered, and Caesar was supreme.

Tragedy pursued the Hasmoneans. After fourteen years as a prisoner in Rome, Aristobulus was poisoned, and his son Alexander executed on Pompey's orders. Only Antigonus was left to challenge Antipater who had transferred his allegiance to Caesar and who was now to reap the reward of years of political expediency. He was made a Roman citizen and Procurator of Judea. Also in the decrees that Caesar issued from Antioch in 47 B.C. he was granted another interesting concession. He was given permission to build a new wall in Jerusalem to protect the temple on the north side.

And it was in this hour of personal triumph that Antipater looked ahead. He succeeded in having Phasael, his eldest son, appointed prefect of Jerusalem, and Herod governor of Galilee. The journey to the Jewish throne for the now twenty-six-year-old Idumean had begun. But four years later his father was dead.

First came the fateful Ides of March, 44 B.C., when Caesar, friend of the Jews, was murdered; a year later Antipater was poisoned at a banquet. It was not long before the Parthians, always a threat to Rome, and alive to the disorder that these events would occasion, were on their way to Jerusalem in support of Antigonus. Their capture of the city resulted in the deportation of Hyrcanus, the suicide of Phasael, and the flight of Herod with his mother and the woman he was to marry, the beautiful, ill-fated Mariamne, daughter of Alexander (son of Aristobulus).

Pursued by Parthians and Jews, Herod turned to fight and beat them at the spot near Bethlehem where he later built the fortress-tomb to which, forty years later, he would be carried on a golden bier. Shaken, but not vanquished by the turn of events, for "the great miseries he was in did not discourage him, but made him sharp in discovering surprising undertakings," Herod went to Rome to plead his case. Antony listened sympathetically, recommended his being made king of the Jews, and the Senate approved the proposal unanimously. Herod had taken another great step forward. He had been given a kingdom, but he still had to win the allegiance of its people and possess its capital. He achieved one of these objectives with the help of the Romans; the other eluded him to his grave.

About a year after his elevation from tetrarch of Galilee to King of Judea, Herod returned to Palestine. The time had come to join issue with Antigonus who was still rallying a nation that was loath to forget its triumphs under the Hasmonean dynasty. There was only one place that the struggle could end. "When the rigour of winter was over, Herod removed his army and came near to Jerusalem, and pitched his camp hard by the city, and came near that part of the wall where it could most easily be assaulted, intending to make his attacks in the same manner as did Pompey."

It was two and a half years since he had fled from the city via the Dung Gate. Now he was to enter it as conqueror and king. But "even while the army lay before the city," Herod betook himself to Samaria where Mariamne was waiting to become his wife after a five-year engagement. The ceremony over, Herod returned to Jerusalem where Sosius, sent by Antony, had arrived with eleven Roman legions, 6,000 horsemen and other auxiliaries out of Syria. There was to be no doubt about the final outcome of this confrontation, however desperate the resistance might prove.

Famine added to the trials of the besieged, for it was a sabbatic year. When the outer walls fell, the defenders retreated to the temple, and finally to the inner court of the sanctuary and the upper city, "until all parts were full of those that were slain, by the rage of the Romans at the long duration of the siege, and by the zeal of the Jews that were on Herod's side." Despite an appeal by Herod himself, "no pity was taken of either infants or of aged, nor did they spare so much as the weaker sex . . . nobody restrained their hand from slaughter, but as if they were a company of madmen, they fell upon persons of all ages, without distinction."

When the senseless slaughter ended at last, Antigonus begged for mercy at the feet of Sosius. It was a vain plea. At Antioch, on the orders of Antony, he was beheaded. "And thus did the government of the Hasmoneans cease, 126 years after it was set up. This family was a splendid and an illustrious one . . . but these men lost the government by their dissensions one with another, and it came to Herod, the son of Antipater . . . one that was subject to other kings."

Herod persuaded Sosius not to plunder or sack the city. He did not want, he said, to be left king of a desert. It was a legitimate request from the man who was to leave not only Jerusalem but many other cities in the land over which he was to rule for another thirty-three years far more splendid than he found them. The year was 37 B.C. and Herod, now thirty-six, was king of the Jews in fact as well as in name.

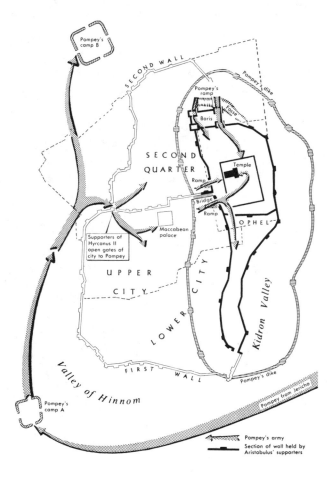

Pompey's siege of Jerusalem (63 B.C.). Josephus wrote that twelve-thousand Jews died in one day during this attack on Jerusalem.

14
Herod's Masterpiece

THERE ARE IN JERUSALEM today, in opposite parts of the city, two hotels with similar names. Survey the scene from the flat rooftop of the Holyland East Hotel and you will become acutely aware of sharp contrasts. Looking south, and not a hundred yards away, are the walls of the Old City; in between, on the highway that leads to Jericho and curves around the base of the Mount of Olives on the east, flows a stream of ceaselessly hooting Arab buses and taxis. Above the walls rises the great gleaming dome of the Muslim shrine, and a little to the right a forest of TV antennae protrude from the humblest of dwellings in the Muslim quarter of the Old City.

The old and the new are existing together.

As they are doing, though in a somewhat different way, at the Holyland Hotel on the crest of a hill in the suburbs of the new city. For here, laid out in a cypress-fringed park, is a model of Jerusalem as it was in the year A.D. 66, four years before it lay in ruins. Built to scale in materials used at the time are the edifices that made it what the elder Pliny called "the most famous of the great cities of the east." Constructions such as the three great towers that protected Herod's magnificent palace: Phasael (whose base is still extant), Mariamne, and Hippicus — named after his brother, his wife, and a friend; the Fortress Antonia, Psephinus, the corner tower of the Third Wall from which, it is said, you could see the Mediterranean on a clear day; and surpassing all, the temple complex "glittering like a snow-capped mountain."

That Herod brought material wealth and prosperity to Jerusalem is plainly evident, but it will always remain something of a mystery why he was able to achieve what not even David had been deemed worthy enough to undertake. To offer to rebuild the Jewish temple was a laudable gesture, but it came from someone who had never ceased to be regarded as a usurper and who had shown himself at times to be nothing less than an implacable tyrant.

Yet Herod succeeded in executing a "work of the greatest piety and excellence that could possibly be undertaken,"[1] as he himself described it. And he did so through characteristic determination, diplomacy, and a certain insight into the tremendous religious significance of the task. Herod knew that the temple was something that set the Jews apart from the rest of the world. It was there that the daily sacrifice had been offered down the centuries and the feasts kept. By making the temple "as complete as he was able,"[2] he would be insuring the full return of God to Jerusalem. But he did not know that before he died there would have entered the world a new High Priest whose teaching would render the temple sacrifice obsolete.

The great project began in the eighteenth year of his reign, 19 B.C. "Knowing that the multitude were not ready nor willing to assist him in so vast a design," Herod tactfully reminded the people that "with God's assistance he had advanced the nations of the Jews to a degree of happiness which they never had before."[3] He told them that what he proposed doing was in the nature of a thank offering for all the blessings that both he and his subjects had enjoyed. He also drew attention to the fact that the existing temple lacked not only a befitting grandeur but also fell short of Solomon's edifice by sixty cubits. These imperfections he desired to correct.

The unique structure required a unique method of construction. Not until everything was ready to be put into position did Herod touch the old building. Ten thousand skilled workmen were chosen for the task; one thousand wagons prepared to carry stones to the site that was enlarged to twice its previous size of some 17 acres by excavations in the north and the building of great retaining walls rising 450 feet from the Kidron Valley on the southeast. Within this area, now measuring 351 yards on the north side, 512 on the east, 536 on the west, and 309 on the south, rose the temple with its Corinthian columns in bronze, its different courts and gates and all encompassed by gleaming, spacious cloisters.

It was Herod's masterpiece, built in the Hellenic style, but he

---

[1]Josephus, *Antiquities of the Jews.*
[2]Ibid.
[3]Ibid.

never saw it completely finished. The sanctuary itself was completed in eighteen months, during which time rain, it is said, fell only at night, and the outer enclosure was finished seven years later. But work on other parts continued until A.D. 64 when already the shadow of destruction had fallen across it.

What irony lay at the heart of this venture! Though the most splendid, it lasted the shortest length of time of all Herod's creations. It was the building to which the Child he attempted to kill was brought to be dedicated, which Christ would deem sacred, and call His Father's house of prayer. It was the temple to which the Messiah would come, and where He would teach, but which He would replace. Like the life of its architect, its life would overlap a new dispensation. Even before its destruction all that it stood for had been superseded and Stephen the first martyr, had declared that "the Most High dwelleth not in temples made with hands" (Acts 7:48).

It was King Herod the Great who fashioned Jerusalem in her last hour of splendor. But within seventy-odd years of his death, her glory lay in the dust. The first disciples had already turned aside from the building that had been the center of worship for a thousand years, and were preaching a new truth in the synagogues and elsewhere. Out of the blackness of its night was to go forth from Jerusalem a light to the Gentiles and to the furthermost part of the world. Already at Antioch a new word had been heard. They were calling the followers of a new religion in which there was neither Jew nor Greek, bond nor free, Christians.

Scale replica of Herod's palace and towers.

15
An Upper Room

Two views of the Coenaculum (dining hall), the place where Jesus supposedly ate the last supper with his disciples. The present structure was built by the crusaders in the twelfth century.

ON ONE OF THE HIGHEST parts of Jerusalem, known long ago as the upper city and today as Mount Zion, there is a large, cool room, reached by climbing some twenty exterior steps. Lying above what is reputed to be the Tomb of David, the room is mercifully empty, graced only by four or five pillars and Byzantine arches. It is as good a place as any and better than most to try to recall a Jerusalem that had come to the most crucial crossroads of its already long history.

For it is the traditional site of the Last Supper. To a room similar to this perhaps, there came, on the eve of His betrayal, the King whom Herod tried to kill, to celebrate the Passover with twelve of His followers. Earlier two of these had been sent into the city from the Mount of Olives to make preparations for the visit. Led by a "man bearing a pitcher of water," they had found the guest-chamber, the "large upper room, furnished and prepared." And they had made ready for the meal (Mark 14:12-16).

It was a desperately sad occasion. It was the last time the little company would meet with its Leader still a free person. The net was spread out to trap Him. The brief, momentous years of His ministry were over. After the first communion and after they had sung a hymn, they would go out into the night to the Garden of Geth-semane, and He would say to James and John and Peter who could not watch one hour with him: "Sleep on now, and take your rest . . . the hour is at hand and the Son of man is betrayed into the hands of sinners" (Matt. 26:45). It was from this place, one might say, perhaps, that the Via Dolorosa began, rather than from the judgment hall of the Palace of Antonia.

107

But if tradition can be trusted, this upper chamber known as the Coenaculum since Roman times (in Latin, "dining hall") has other less-tragic associations that those of the betrayal eve. It was, it would seem, the upstairs part of the house of Mary, mother of John whose surname was Mark, where Peter came after the angel had flung open his prison doors, and where Thomas was given proof of the risen Lord.

Here on the Feast of Pentecost had gathered in quiet expectation that valiant company of Hebrew believers, for had not the Master promised a Comforter who would abide for ever once He had gone? "And suddenly," Luke writes, "there came a sound from heaven as of a rushing mighty wind, and it filled all the house where they were sitting . . . and they were all filled with the Holy Spirit" (Acts 2:2,4). Nearby in the temple, still standing in all its splendor, the priests were offering up the daily sacrifice, unaware that it was no longer necessary.

Fifty days before, a Jerusalem crowded to capacity had, it thought, disposed of another usurper, another troublemaker from Galilee. To the question that John the Baptist had put from his dungeon in the fortress at Macherus — "Art thou he that should come, or look we for another?" (Luke 7:19) — the city had given its own answer. To its long and amazing saga it had added the most amazing fact of all. In a moment of time it had cut down the desire of the ages, the desire of those living in bondage and hope. With desperate haste it had conducted within its walls the greatest mistrial in history, denied the Holy One and the Just, and pardoned a murderer instead. When power from on high had come upon the group in the upper room, the holy city had not begun to understand that the earth was no longer the same, that its Creator had walked upon it in the form of Man, had healed its sick and instituted a New Covenant. It could not know that, beginning with Jerusalem, and within the lifetime of Paul the apostle to the Gentiles, the faith of those it would kill and persecute would go to the uttermost parts of the Roman world. Though it would be told it had killed the Prince of Life, it would not believe. With a stubbornness and perversity born of old, it would go on stoning those sent to it and rejecting the things that belonged to its peace.

It was Jerusalem that Christ always knew He would one day have to face alone, where in His hour of trial "as a sheep before her shearers is dumb," He would open not His mouth (Isa. 53:7). Jerusalem in all its formalism and hypocrisy would be the last place He would visit, as it was the first. It was to the glittering temple of Herod that Mary, "when the days of her purification according to the law of Moses were accomplished," brought her forty-day-old child "to be presented to the Lord." The presentation was accompanied by an offering of two turtle doves, the humblest gift, permitted only to the poor. But nobody was taking much notice of the family of Joseph, a carpenter from a despised village called Nazareth. Except two rather special people — the just and devout Simeon, content to die now that he had seen the longed-for Messiah, and eighty-four-year-old Anna, a prophetess who also rejoiced in her recognition of the promised Redeemer (Luke 2:22-38).

A fleeting glimpse and then the silence of twelve years falls across the Life that had made its first contact with Jerusalem. Egypt becomes a haven until Herod is dead; of the boyhood years in the home in Nazareth there is merely conjecture. We know for certain only that "the child grew and waxed strong in spirit" (Luke 2:40). That this was so the next scene clearly shows, for Jesus is again in the temple, but this time He is in "the midst of the doctors, both hearing them, and asking them questions" (Luke 2:46).

Jerusalem, suddenly, is now beyond doubt the Holy City, for the Holy One of God is there, "busy about his Father's business." But with the return to Nazareth the curtain is drawn once more, this time for eighteen years, during which time we know again only that Jesus "grew in wisdom and stature and in favour with God and man" (Luke 2:52) in preparation for those things that began "in the fifteenth year of the reign of Tiberius Caesar," when Herod Antipas was tetrarch of Galilee, Pontius Pilate was governor of Judea, and John was preaching the baptism of repentance in the country round about Jordan. And when Jesus Himself "began to be about thirty years of age" and John saw the heavens opened and the Holy Spirit descending on Him like a dove (Luke 3:21-23).

The days of obscurity were over, for the beloved Son in whom God was well pleased was ready for the task that lay ahead. From now on every step He took and every word He uttered would be carefully noted. And changes would be of a tremendous nature. Even Jerusalem would no longer be Herod's Jerusalem, as it was Nehemiah's and Solomon's and David's. It would be the Jerusalem now of the Gospels, the city at first of Jesus, the Nazarene teacher and healer, before it became the Jerusalem of the Christ who would suffer and rise from the dead on the third day.

The temple would no longer be Herod's. It would be the sanctuary to which Satan would bring the Son of God from the wilderness to tempt Him, from where the money-changers would be driven, and which Jesus would make sacred with His presence. As long as He was there, the city and the temple would be safe. But once He had gone nothing could save them.

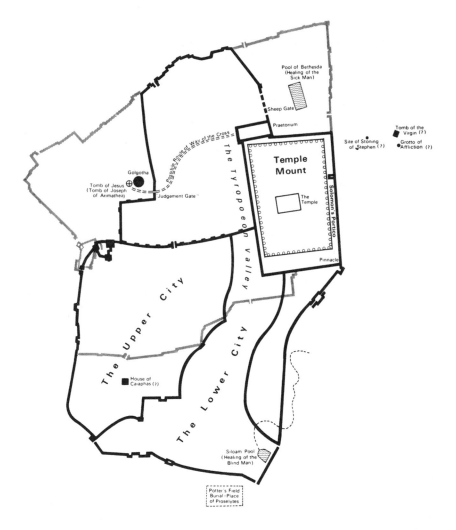

Jerusalem in the time of Jesus.

16
The Last Journey

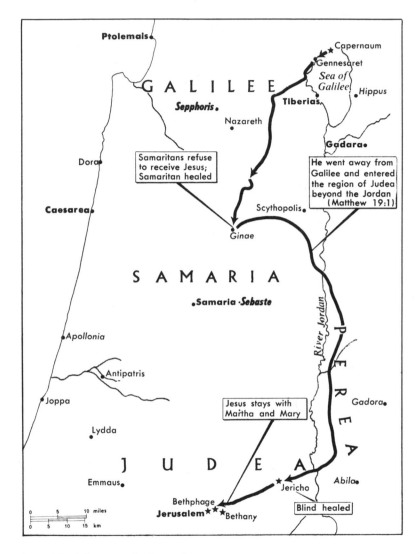

Ptolemais•

Capernaum

•Gennesaret

Sea of
Galilee

•Hippus

GALILEE

Sepphoris •

Tiberias•

•Nazareth

Gadara•

Dora•

| Samaritans refuse |
| to receive Jesus; |
| Samaritan healed |

| He went away from |
| Galilee and entered |
| the region of Judea |
| beyond the Jordan |
| (Matthew 19:1) |

Caesarea•

Scythopolis•

•Ginae

S A M A R I A

•Samaria ·*Sebaste*

•Apollonia

River Jordan

P
E
R
E
A

•Antipatris

•Joppa

| Jesus stays with |
| Martha and Mary |

Gadora•

•Lydda

J U D E A

•Emmaus

Abila•

★Jericho

| Blind healed |

Bethphage
Jerusalem★ ★
★Bethany

| 0 | 5 | 10 miles |
| 0 | 5 | 10 | 15 km |

Jesus' last journey to Jerusalem.

The last pilgrimage of the Prophet of Nazareth to Jerusalem was climaxed with the messianic shout "Blessed is he that cometh in the name of the Lord."

"HE STEADFASTLY SET his face to go to Jerusalem" (Luke 9:51). There is a significance in these few words that can never be fully assessed, for they mark the beginning of the last stage of God's walk in the flesh with man. In an instant the whole forbidding nature of the now imminent climax to the earthly ministry is set before us. Indeed, there is expressed in this simple statement the whole essence of the Christian evangel — the necessity for a vicarious sacrifice at great and terrible cost. The road to Jerusalem, this time, led to the Cross.

The last journeys through Samaria, through Galilee, around Capernaum, and to the borders of Tyre and Sidon had been made; the days of preaching to the multitude beside the incomparable lake were over. The disciples had been chosen, the seventy sent out; the Transfiguration had taken place. Far up at Caesarea Philippi at the foot of snow-capped Mount Hermon, He had tested His closest followers with the question: "But whom say ye that I am?" (Matt. 16:15), and Peter had made his historic affirmation concerning the divinity of Christ.

The sparkling waters still gush out of the ground at this place in the Golan Heights, from where the Syrians were driven in the Six-Day War, and flow as a tributary to the Jordan. But the town that Tetrarch Philip enlarged and named in honor of Tiberius Caesar and himself has long since gone. Once the center bore the Greek name Panias, because the Greek god Pan was worshiped there, and this is what the Arabs call it today. But they spell it Banias, because there is no *p* in the Arabic alphabet. Just above the spring there are several inscribed niches carved in the cliff — all that remains now of a sanctuary once dedicated to the god of herds and pastures.

It is perhaps significant that Peter's attestation to the divinity of his Lord was made in the heart of paganism. It marked a notable stage in the preparation of the apostles for the dark and critical days that were ahead. From now on, the road lay only south to Jerusalem, to a Jewry that sought His death (John 7:1). Previously when they would have laid hands on Him, He had passed through their midst, for His time had not yet come. But now it would be different; they would be permitted to have their own way with Him.

On this last journey from Galilee, the little company was refused permission to go through Samaria, and so they went by way of the "borders of Judea and beyond Jordan," the strange river that twists and turns in its wide gorge seven hundred feet below sea level for two hundred miles, trying to escape its bitter fate in the Dead Sea and whose twenty-seven rapids render it unnavigable. Fourteen hundred and fifty years before, its waters "had risen up in a heap" to allow the Israelites under Joshua "to pass over on dry ground" (Josh. 3:16,17). In it, after dipping himself seven times, Naaman was cleansed of his leprosy; to it Jesus had come to be baptized of John, and over it He now crossed for the last time, making His way to Jericho.

There were still some twenty miles to go, and the highway was thronged with Galileans flocking to the Holy City for Passover week. It was to be indeed another memorable day for the oldest city in the world, whose walls had once collapsed at a shout and the blowing of trumpets. It was a day that sight came to the blind and salvation to the home of Zacchaeus. It was the day Bartimaeus also triumphed by a shout. He had sensed that something unusual was happening and when told "Jesus of Nazareth passeth by" (Luke 18:37), had made himself heard above the multitude in his cry to be healed. Zacchaeus, being small of stature, had to climb a sycamore tree to satisfy his curiosity. But both efforts were handsomely rewarded. That Zacchaeus was rich is not surprising. He was chief publican, or tax gatherer, in a city whose balsam groves were famous and lucrative. Mark Antony had once given them as a present to Cleopatra, who in turn had leased them to Herod the Great at a substantial figure. When the latter built a palace here and made it his winter capital, "all Palestine," it was said, was "not to be compared with Jericho for sheer luxury." Here, in this city of palms, where Elisha once purified the springs, Herod died a few months after Jesus was born.

And here in the home of Zacchaeus Jesus spent the night before He set out on the stretch of mountainous road that was the locale for His parable of the Good Samaritan. The uphill track that led from the historic oasis sunk eight hundred feet in the humid desolation of the Jordan Valley, up through the forbidding crags of the Judean wilderness to the city that was waiting menacingly "that all things the prophets had written concerning the Son of man might be accomplished" (Luke 18:31).

But there was still Bethany and Bethphage and the acclamations on the slope of Mount Olivet of those who remembered "all the mighty works they had seen" (Luke 19:37). There was yet to ring through the streets of Jerusalem the shout "Blessed is he that cometh in the name of the Lord" as the multitude spread their garments and strewed the branches of trees in the way of the ass bearing the Prophet of Nazareth of Galilee. But even while the air was still filled with the crowd's hosannas, the chief priests and the scribes and elders would be consulting together how "they might take Jesus by subtlety and kill him" (Matt. 26:4).

Century after century history had been moving slowly but steadily in a certain direction. The nation that had been chosen to usher into the world a Savior "to all them that believe" had done so in the fullness of time. He had dwelt among them and every prophecy concerning Him had been fulfilled. Nothing remained now but the swift advance to the awful climax. Suddenly Rome and all the leaders of Jewry found themselves for once united in an unholy alliance. Together they would succeed in perpetrating the greatest act of injustice the world has ever seen. "This was their hour and the power of darkness" (Luke 22:53).

17
The Saddest Walk

Ancient olive tree in the Garden of Gethsemane. There are eight of these old olive trees in the garden, and they may be as much as three-thousand years old. Josephus records that Titus cut down all the trees around Jerusalem in A.D. 70. It is possible that these trees in the garden may have escaped destruction; but if not, they may well be the shoots of those trees Jesus may have prayed under in the garden.

YOU MAY STAND in the land that is Israel today and see changes that make this the most transformed country in the world. Or you may stand beside the lake of Galilee and feel that in 2,000 years nothing has changed at all. There are still only small fishing boats on its shimmering blue surface. Just visible through the haze are the Jordanian hills on the opposite shore. And there in the lee of a little mound of sand are shadows, figures mending their nets and mingling with the soft lapping of the waters their cry of astonishment, "What manner of man is this that even the winds and the sea obey him!" (Matt. 8:27).

Here in the half-light of evening and in the noonday heat mists, the happenings of long ago unfold with perfect ease. Time has stopped on these shores, as it does perhaps at all those places that man does not touch. But it is not only because this lovely sheet of water has not changed that you may look on it and marvel. It is because you are suddenly aware that you are looking at the lake He rebuked and stilled and on which He walked. No one has been able to alter what was here when Peter one day began to sink beneath the waves and cried out, " 'Lord, save me!' and immediately Jesus stretched forth his hand and caught him" (Matt. 14:30,31). There are no ornate doors to this hallowed place, no stained glass windows; it has no marble steps or golden dome, only the arch of heaven for its roof; and the stars at night are its sole custodians.

It was from here and the peaceful country round about that Jesus went up to Jerusalem after three momentous years. At any time there is a contrast between Jerusalem set high on its Judean hills and Galilee, that has to be seen and felt if it is to be

119

properly understood. But the contrast that it must have presented to Christ on that final visit no one could fully understand. The grim ramparts of the fortress-city must have assumed an even more sinister appearance, epitomizing the inflexibility that has been part and parcel of Jerusalem's makeup since the beginning. Never could the city have seemed so intolerable and menacing in its outward appearance, and one that was to be matched soon by the spirit within.

And it was within these imprisoning walls that Christ knew only too well that His final confrontation with the authorities, now united by a common purpose, had to take place. "Behold, the world is gone after him!"the Pharisees had cried in alarm (John 12:19). And He had likened them to "whited sepulchres" and to "blind guides who strained at a gnat and swallowed a camel" (Matt. 23:24,27), who had omitted the weightier matters of the law like mercy and faith, whose works were done to be seen of men, and who did not practice what they preached. This time, Christ knew, they were determined to make an end of Him.

Why Jesus had to "steadfastly set his face towards Jerusalem" from far-off Capernaum and beyond becomes clearer with every step He took in the closing hours of His life. There was not a move that did not increase His suffering, that did not require a courage that no man will ever equal. He faced the implacable, hostile city, in whose temple He had preached, in whose streets He had performed miracles, alone. It was in this city that He had challenged and denounced the Pharisees. Though He had spoken often to His disciples of the things that were to happen to Him, they had "understood none of them." They could not even stay awake with Him in Gethsemane, and when He was arrested, "they all forsook him and fled" (Matt. 26:56). In the city over which He had wept only a few days before, every hand was now against Him — from that of Judas to that of another Herod. Resolution of a supreme nature had indeed been necessary for such an encounter.

On the Tuesday He had visited the temple for the last time, cleansing it of the moneychangers and later foretelling its destruction to the amazed disciples; He had answered the chief priests who had tried to trap Him that they should "render unto Caesar the things that are Caesar's and unto God the things that are God's" (Matt. 22:21); and He had delivered His great Olivet discourse on what was to happen in the last days. And every night that last fateful week "he went out and abode in the mount that is called the mount of Olives" (Luke 21:37).

Until "the feast of unleavened bread, which is called the passover, drew nigh" (Luke 22:1).

The saddest walk in all history was the one that Jesus took when He left the upper room, possibly about eight o'clock, after His last meal with the twelve disciples, and passed over the brook Kidron into Gethsemane. It was the last walk He was free, the last He took with His closest followers, the one before which He had uttered that cry of inexpressible anguish: "Now is my soul troubled; and what shall I say? Father, save me from this hour: but for this cause came I unto this hour" (John 12:27). There had followed the washing of His disciples' feet in the upper room, the giving of the sop to Judas who went out into the night to act the traitor, the declaration to Peter that he would deny his Lord three times before morning.

It was in those last few moments He had in the Passover chamber with a perplexed and downcast eleven that Jesus spoke some of the most comforting and most profound words in the Bible. He was going, He told them, to prepare a place that where He was they might be also; that He was the way, the truth, and the life; and that no one could come to the Father except through Him; that a Comforter would be sent who would guide them into all truth. He told them not to be afraid and promised them His peace, and not as the world gives. Then He had said, "Arise, let us go hence," and so began the last walk to a garden where "he had oft times resorted with his disciples" (John 18:2). It was dark. Those who were with Him were not sure what was going to happen next, but Jesus knew He had a rendezvous with death.

But there was still much to be said, and as the little group made its way slowly through the city to one of the gates opening on to the Kidron Valley, Jesus warned His disciples of the hard times ahead, that the hour had now come, in fact, when they would be scattered and tribulation would be their lot. Because they had been "chosen out of this world," the world would hate them, but they were to be of good cheer, for He had overcome the world. They would be sorrowful, but their sorrow would turn to joy when they saw and knew that He had risen from the dead. Because they had loved Him and had believed that He had come from God, whatever they asked the Father in His name would, in the days to come, be given them.

They had reached the crossing over the stream. The garden was a few yards away. Almost the last words to His disciples had been spoken, but there remained still that great prayer of intercession for those God had given Him, who should not be taken out of the world but kept from evil in it, and that He should be glorified as the Son with a glory that He had with God before the world began, because He had finished the work He had been given to do (John 17). And then, last of all, before the soldiers came, and while Peter, James, and John slept, that cry to the Father while He sweat, as it were great drops of blood: "If it be possible, let this cup pass from me; nevertheless not as I will, but as thou wilt" (Matt. 26:39; Luke 22:44).

But even as He prayed and an angel was strengthening Him, those with swords and staves were on their way to the garden, because, on returning to the still slumbering disciples the third time, He said, "Rise, let us be going: behold, he is at hand that doth betray me" (Matt. 26:46).

The moment for surrender had come. What Judas had had to do, he had done quickly; the trap was now sprung. The travesty that was to be regarded as a trial was about to commence. Within a few hours God would have to turn the day into night because of what man had done to His Son. But in the midst of the awful picture that Jerusalem was now to present, there stands the incomparable Christ, calm and majestic, as He faces His accusers, unresisting to every abuse. The target of treachery, violence, hate, and ridicule, He is moved only to compassion and love.

In the flickering light of the torches and lanterns He assures those sent by the captains of the temple and elders to apprehend Him in the garden that He is Jesus of Nazareth, the person for whom they are looking. And His next thought is for His disciples, for He adds: "I have told you that I am he; if therefore ye seek me, let these go their way" (John 18:8). The ear of Malchus, the servant of the high priest, is immediately restored, and the impetuous Peter is told to put his sword back in its sheath, "for all that take the sword shall perish with it" [Matt. 26:52]. The use of force is condemned, and the disciple is quietly reminded of the power of the One in whose presence he is standing: "Thinkest thou that I cannot now pray to my Father, and he shall presently give me more than twelve legions of angels?" (Matt. 26:53). And also of the cause for which the Son of man came into the world: "The cup which my Father hath given me, shall I not drink it?" (John 18:11).

Back along the path that He had just walked freely though

sorrowfully with His disciples, Jesus now goes bound and in the midst of enemies. Those who would make the first moves in a trial that was to be devoid of every vestige of justice had been alerted and were waiting for Him.

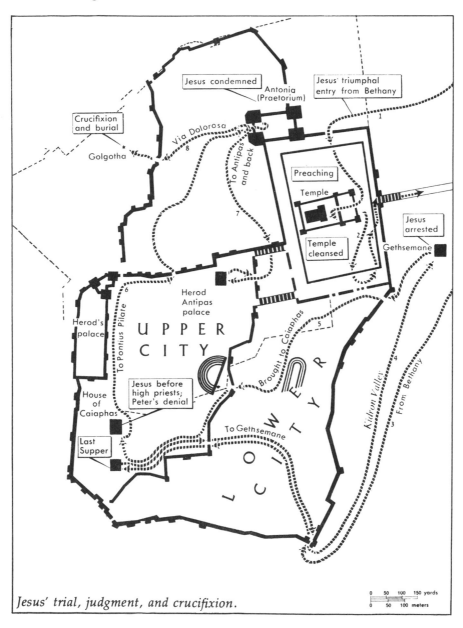

Jesus' trial, judgment, and crucifixion.

18
Rendevous With Death

W HAT HAPPENED IN JERUSALEM in those next few terrible hours cannot be attributed solely to the machinations of Christ's own race. The trial that began as an ecclesiastical one in the house of Annas ended in a Roman court with the charge against the accused being changed from one of blasphemy to one of treason. From the time of the arrest in Gethsemane to the verdict of Pilate, conformity of the proceedings either with Jewish or Roman law was virtually nonexistent. They were, in fact, in every way a travesty of not only legal, but even humanitarian, principles.

Gentile complicity in the death of Christ is as clear and as irrefutable as the Jewish plotting and promotion of it. Jesus Himself disclosed that He would be delivered into the hands of the Gentiles, and be mocked and spitefully entreated and spit on; and they would scourge Him and put Him to death, and the third day He would rise again (Luke 18:32,33). Luke adds a further testimony: "For of a truth against thy holy child Jesus, whom thou hast anointed, both Herod and Pontius Pilate, with the Gentiles, and the people of Israel, were gathered together, for to do whatsoever thy hand and thy counsel determined before to be done" (Acts 4:27,28).

Nor can blame be apportioned in one direction more than in another. When the Sanhedrin sought the death penalty, the case passed beyond their jurisdiction because they had been deprived of the right of capital punishment. It was in the power of both Pilate and Herod Antipas to have set Jesus free. The former declared four times that Jesus was innocent, and Herod found "nothing worthy of death" in Him (Luke 23:15). The final say in the whole matter lay with Pilate. There was no higher structure of justice in the Gentile

127

world than a Roman court; Pilate was a Roman judge and it was Roman soldiers who assaulted Christ and carried out the crucifixion, a Roman not a Jewish form of execution.

No amount of emphasis on the insistence of the Jews in this matter can ever excuse the Roman governor for his weakness. Pilate had not the slightest justification for handing over for death someone whom he had found innocent of any crime. The Jews for their part were guilty in that they demanded the death sentence for one in whom there had been found no offense. Although they did not believe that Christ was the Messiah, they had been given ample proof that He was.

From the very outset, of course, Jesus knew that the Jewish hierarchy would not let Him escape this time. Beneath the sanctimonious air of shock it expressed at His statements that He was the Son of God was the far more bitter resentment of His exposure of Pharisaical hypocrisy. The challenge to their authority could no longer be tolerated. And so began their controversy with the Holy One of Israel.

While violation of Jewish law began even before the apprehension of Jesus with the offer of Judas to betray Him to the priests, three irregularities, at least, occurred in Gethsemane that would have gained any other prisoner his release: the arrest took place after sundown, no formal charges were laid, and members of the court that later sat in judgment on Christ could have been among the crowd that accompanied the soldiers. These were all ignored and the first stage of the trial began illegally at night and on the eve of the Feast of Unleavened Bread before Annas, a former high priest, and father-in-law of Caiaphas.

Again no charges were made, and Annas violated the law by conducting this part of the proceedings on his own and acting, not simply as a judge, but as a prosecutor. Questioned quite unethically on His doctrine, Jesus simply replied, "In secret have I said nothing. Why askest thou me? Ask them which heard me . . . they know what I said" (John 18:20,21). For this He was struck by an officer — another breach of law.

Annas then sent Jesus bound to Caiaphas and the travesty of justice continued when a committee of the Sanhedrin met illegally in his house for a night session. In the absence of both formal indictment and the chief witness for the prosecution, Judas Iscariot, false witnesses were sought to give evidence. When this move failed,

Caiaphas, president of the Sanhedrin, in blatant disregard of legal procedure, challenged Jesus himself: "Tell us," he said, "whether thou be the Christ, the Son of God" (Matt. 26:63).

Under oath, Christ's answer in the affirmative was the one used to convict Him of blasphemy, but legally the conviction was indefensible because it was forced self-incrimination, and no person could rightly be condemned on His own testimony. Caiaphas went further in his unethical conduct by asking for a verbal opinion from the assembly: "What further need have we of witnesses? Behold, now ye have heard his blasphemy. What think ye?" (Matt. 26:65,66).

"They answered and said, He is guilty of death. Then did they spit in his face, and buffeted him, and others smote him with the palms of their hands" (Matt. 26:66,67).

Such treatment of a prisoner was unheard of, while the very fact that the verdict of "guilty" was unanimous legally entitled the accused to an acquittal because in such circumstances Jews considered the prisoner had not had a fair trial.

In a trial involving the possible pronouncement of the death sentence it was always customary to allow a night to elapse before such a judgment was given. This rule was not observed and the meeting of the full council of the Sanhedrin was illegally convened at dawn on the first day of the Feast of Unleavened Bread. Again, in the absence of any witnesses, Christ was wrongfully compelled to bear testimony against Himself, was condemned for blasphemy, and "when they had bound him, they led him away and delivered him to Pontius Pilate, the governor" (Matt. 27:2).

It is in his favor that Pilate refused to condemn Jesus out of hand, and three charges were then advanced against Him by the Jews. "We found this fellow perverting the nation, and forbidding to give tribute to Caesar, saying that he himself is Christ a King" (Luke 23:2). Only the charge of treason interested Pilate, but in the face of Christ's reply that His kingdom was not of this world and that every one who is of the truth hears His voice (John 18:36,37), he was forced to declare that he found no fault in the accused at all.

The Roman governor, however, was continuing the irregularities of the Jewish trials by not calling for witnesses against the accused, by conducting the trial without a jury, and by seeking incriminating evidence from the prisoner Himself. On his findings at this point, Jesus should have been released. Instead, on being told by the incensed crowd that Jesus had "stirred up" the people beginning at Galilee (Luke 23:5), he seized on what he thought was a way out of his dilemma. He sent Jesus to Herod Antipas, tetrarch of Galilee, who was in Jerusalem at the time.

And so He who escaped the murderous hand of Herod the Great came face to face with his son, the slayer of John the Baptist. It was a meeting that Antipas had long wanted, and he now hoped that his curiosity would be satisfied with the performing of some miracle by the Galilean. But when Jesus "answered him nothing," his hurt pride soon manifested itself in a mocking of the prisoner. But this was as far as Herod Antipas went. Herod "arrayed him in a gorgeous robe" and returned Him to Pilate, not having found Him "worthy of death" (Luke 23:11,15).

It is not impossible, perhaps, to feel a slight tinge of sympathy for Pilate at this stage. Twice he had declared Jesus innocent and was, apparently, prepared to release Him. But the insistence and hostility of the Jews was growing, fanned by those in authority. And any sympathy for him must vanish with his next three moves, each of which was taken with the hope of appeasing the crowd. He had Jesus scourged; he allowed Him to be clothed in a purple robe, a crown of thorns to be put on His head, and the soldiers to ridicule Him in a mock coronation; and he offered to release Him instead of a man "that for sedition and murder was cast into prison" (Luke 13:25).

None of these totally illegal acts, made even more reprehensible by further protestations by Pilate of Jesus' innocence, were of any use. The cries "Crucify him, crucify him!" from outside the judgment hall merely became louder and more urgent. And it was then that Pilate, amazed at the silence of Jesus, asked Him, "Knowest thou not that I have power to crucify thee, and have power to release thee?" (John 19:10).

And this time Jesus spoke, and said, "Thou couldest have no power at all against me, except it were given thee from above" (John 19:11). The words made Pilate even more anxious to release his prisoner, but there was to be no way out for him because the Jews then played their winning card.

"If thou let this man go," they said, "thou art not Caesar's friend; whosoever maketh himself a king speaketh against Caesar" (John 19:12).

Pilate was trapped. The words of the Jews were the epitome of hypocrisy, but they were highly effective. The trial that had been a mockery from the start was over, for now that Pilate's own safety was at stake, there was no hope for Jesus. Pilate himself was now on trial, and he had no intention of taking any chances. When the people shouted, "Away with him, away with him, crucify him," Pilate, in a last desperate but futile gesture, asked, "Shall I crucify your King?" And the people gave their fateful, blasphemous answer: "We have no king but Caesar. His blood be on us, and on our children" (John 19:15; Matt. 27:25).

Then Pilate, in a final dramatic gesture, "took water, and washed his hands before the multitude, saying: I am innocent of the blood of this just person: see ye to it" (Matt. 27:24). The demonstration only made what he had already done more inexcusable. He knew that it was because of envy that the Jews were trying to get rid of Jesus; even his wife had warned him, "Have thou nothing to do with that just man" (Matt. 27:19). But he became clay in the hands of the people he both hated and despised, and the instrument by which they achieved their purpose, for in the end "he delivered Jesus to their will" (Luke 23:25).

It was nearly nine o'clock on the day before the Passover Sabbath. Less than twelve hours had elapsed since Jesus had been arrested, and an incredible number of things had happened in that time. Jewry had resolved that their adversary must be out of the way before the start of the Sabbath and they had left no stone unturned in their efforts to achieve this goal. As it happened, they had three hours to spare.

By three o'clock that afternoon the rejected Messiah had been put to death and men's hands were stained by the blackest deed of all time. However, for most who either witnessed or took part in the proceedings that day, nothing very unusual had happened. A Galilean and two thieves had paid the supreme penalty for certain alleged crimes. True, there had been a disturbance in the heavens and an unnatural darkness for three hours, and the earth had shaken, but such events could be explained, and things had then continued as they were before.

But as the light of a new dispensation spread across the earth, men began to talk of Jerusalem as the city of the Crucifixion. And they did so uncritically and with growing fervor and a strange sense of indebtedness to what had taken place there. The event had begun to assume tremendous significance, *for the infamy of the cross now became associated with the secret of man's eternal destiny.*

19
"There Was a Garden"

A garden tomb like that of Joseph's, now part of the Church of the Holy Sepulchre.

STAND FOR A MOMENT at the Damascus Gate on practically any day of the year and the world will pass before you in an ever-changing stream of humanity. Here East meets West and the centuries vanish in a few paces. The old city walls extend on either side of you and there comes the thought: Was this the gate that Christ passed through on His way to Golgotha?

In the words of one of the best-known hymns in the English language, the place where Jesus laid down His life was

> . . . a green hill far away,
> Without a city wall. . . .

It was, we are sure, outside a city wall, because the writer to the Hebrews says, "Wherefore Jesus also, that he might sanctify the people with his own blood, suffered without the gate" (13:12). But was it on a hill? Nowhere do the Gospels specifically state that it was.

They all tell us, in slightly different words that "He bearing his cross went forth into a place called the place of a skull, which is called in the Hebrew Golgotha, where they crucified him" (John 19:17,18).

Two thousand years ago this was the official execution site of the Romans. It may have derived its name from this fact or because it resembled a human skull. It was located outside the walls of Jerusalem but fairly close to the city and, in conformity with the practice of the Romans, most likely on a public highway. And in this instance on a height. For the Hebrew is a rendering of the Greek *kranion,* and the name implies the summit of a skull-like mound or moderate hill. The now commonly accepted and hallowed word *Calvary* used only

135

once, in Luke, is a version of *calvarius* ("bald skull") from the Latin Vulgate.

But where is Calvary today — and the empty tomb? The lake, Olivet, the temple mount, Galilee, Samaria, the Jordan, the Kidron Valley, and even Gethsemane, are all there in recognizable form. But is there that which would tend to remind us of the place where Jesus went when He left the judgment hall of Pilate? The Bible tells us that "in the place where he was crucified there was a garden; and in the garden a new sepulchre, wherein was never man yet laid. There laid they Jesus" (John 19:41,42).

Those responsible for this kindly act were Joseph of Arimathaea, "an honourable counsellor," whose tomb it was, and Nicodemus, he who "at the first came to Jesus by night." Both were members of the Sanhedrin but held no brief for its recent actions. And they came now to prepare the body for burial, with the linen and the "mixture of myrrh and aloes, about a hundred pound weight" that Nicodemus had brought (Mark 15:43; John 19:39).

The terrible six hours were over. Jesus had died sooner than expected, for Pilate was surprised when Joseph asked if he could take the body away. On that awful last walk when Jesus had made His way to Calvary — a walk that was but a continuation of the one begun the night before — He told the daughters of Jerusalem to weep for themselves and for their children (Luke 23:28). On the crest of the hill that must have been anything but green, one of the malefactors who had said to the other, "We receive the due reward of our deeds: but this man hath done nothing amiss" (Luke 23:41), had been received into Paradise; the soldiers had shared His clothing and cast lots for His coat that was without seam; Mary had been committed into the care of the "beloved" disciple.

At noon (the sixth hour) when the sun was at its zenith in the sky, darkness had hidden the crosses from men's gaze, the earth had trembled, and the veil of the temple had been rent from the top to the bottom. And at the ninth hour there had been uttered the most tragic, the most awe-inspiring words this world has ever heard: "Eli, Eli, lama sabachthani? that is to say, My God, my God, why hast thou forsaken me?" (Matt. 27:46). And then, when He had received the vinegar, with His last breath He uttered that final cry of triumph: "It is finished" (John 19:30).

In order to bring on death more quickly so that the bodies could be removed from the crosses before the Sabbath began, the Jews had asked that the legs of the victims be broken. But when the soldiers had come to Jesus, they found Him already dead and, instead, one of them pierced His side with a spear, thus fulfilling Old Testament prophecies to the letter.

Thus do the Gospel writers describe in simple, unadorned language the event that divided history in two, that was to change the whole pattern of man's religious concepts and bring him into a completely new and different relationship with God.

Nowhere in the whole account of the Crucifixion is there the slightest hint of overdramatization of a form of death that nothing else equalled in the intensity of suffering endured by the victim. Where there could easily have been repellent details, there is only a remarkable and terribly effective silence. But enough is always said to convey the awfulness of the ordeal and to bear accurate witness to all that the prophets had written concerning it centuries before.

And it is John who tells us that "in the place where Jesus was crucified there was a garden" (John 19:41). There is something peculiarly significant about this piece of information. Man began his long sojourn on earth in a garden, Christ spent many hours in the garden on the Mount of Olives, and heaven itself could be a garden. This one could very well have been at the base of the Crucifixion hillock, for it "was near by," with the newly hewn sepulcher in the cliff face where it was customary to place tombs.

Is there such a place in Jerusalem today? Strangely enough, there is, but tradition does not recognize it as Golgotha. It lies, according to tradition, beneath one of the many lamp-lit chapels within the Church of the Holy Sepulcher, the holy site being shared by the Latins and the Greeks. It is reached by ascending some twenty well-worn stone steps, but of any hill there is no sign. Below is the Catholicon, the Greek Cathedral in the middle of which is a stone chalice said to mark the center of the earth; next to it and immediately beneath the church's high dome stands a tiny and much-ornamented structure containing a marble grave.

For over 1,600 years this complex of shrines has been accepted as marking Christendom's holiest sites, and from this distance in time who is to say for sure that it does not? But there are doubts, and a regret that what you had pictured in your mind has here been marred. But cast your net a little wider for a reminder of that far-off day and you will find it, perhaps, in the only place in Jerusalem that is said to have borne, and still bears, the name "Skull Hill."

It rises outside the city wall some two hundred yards northeast of the Damascus Gate at the end of a narrow lane leading off the Nablus Road. This is Arab Jerusalem, crammed with a multitude of tiny shops radiating out from a bus terminal. A Muslim cemetery now straddles the crest of the rocky eminence beyond, giving it a striking resemblance to a human skull, and at the base of it there is an opening in the cliff face with shrubs and flowers growing in the surrounding area. This is the Garden Tomb, also known as Gordon's Calvary.

Though he was not the first to entertain the idea that this might conceivably be Golgotha, it was on further investigation by General Charles Gordon, hero of Khartoum, that stronger credence to the possibility was given. The clearing away of the rubble had revealed the existence of a Roman tomb cut in the solid rock face. The tomb was divided into two sections and had several unusual features. As well as receiving light from the open doorway, it was lit by a window placed in such a way that a shaft of light penetrated at dawn to the farthest wall and fell on one of the two graves in the chamber. This, it is reasoned, could account for the disciples being able to see, without actually entering it, that the sepulcher was empty that Easter morning. At the foot of this particular grave, the stone had been cut away to give added length. This was a unique feature and suggested that someone taller than Joseph of Arimathaea had at the last moment been laid there. The rock had also been hewn in such a way as to provide a seat at both ends of the grave bed, and this could explain how Mary Magdalene had seen, when she stooped down, "two angels in white sitting, the one at the head, and the other at the feet, where the body of Jesus had lain" (John 20:12).

Further supporting evidence that this could have been the tomb of Joseph is advanced in the fact that a shrine stone of Venus, traces of a building that had been erected over the tomb, and two recesses characteristic of Venus temples above the tomb's entrance, were discovered. These are relics, it is held, of the shrine built by Hadrian over the tomb to humiliate the early Christians.

It is also believed that "Skull Hill" is a continuation of Mount Moriah, being its southern end. The abrupt face of the hill is the result of a moat cut by the Maccabees to keep their enemies at bay, and few realize that Golgotha was at one time connected with the northern portion of Mount Moriah on which the temple was built. Moriah was the scene of Abraham's preparation for the sacrifice of Isaac. Calvary was enacted there, in type. Later, at the same spot when "an angel of the Lord stood by the threshing floor of Araunah the Jebusite," judgment on Jerusalem had been stayed. At Golgotha, judgment on the believer was canceled. On the threshing floor David built an altar; at Golgotha stood a cross, on which was offered the supreme sacrifice.

Excavations under the Damascus Gate in 1937 revealed the tops of two Roman gates, and appear to confirm the belief that the present north wall follows the line of the second wall and is just where it was in Jesus' day. If this is so, then Golgotha could not have been where the Church of the Holy Sepulcher now stands, for we know it was "without the gate" that Christ suffered.

Which gate it was and where the gate actually stood is not important. That we may never be sure where the tomb of Joseph of Arimathaea lay does not matter. It could, however, have been similar to the one discovered in the side of "Skull Hill," and for this realistic link with the past there can only be a sense of gratification. It is a good deal easier to try to recapture a little of what happened on that glorious resurrection morn in the garden tomb than it is within the crumbling walls of a Crusader church.

But all that really matters is that somewhere in this vicinity there was a cross, and on that Easter morning the tomb in the garden was empty.

20
The New Way

"The Angel at the Sepulchre" by Dore.

*In the ancient city tragedy turned to triumph; a man, indeed the Carpenter of
Nazareth, returned from the dead and showed himself to be the Messiah of whom
the prophets had written.*

I F JERUSALEM HAD BEEN the scene of the Crucifixion only, knowledge of the event would have ceased within fifty years, or even
less. But it was more than that. It was the scene of the Resurrection
and, forty days later, of the Ascension. It was these events that made
all the difference to that burial in a tomb whose entrance was sealed
with a great stone and over which a watch was set. It was the words
of the angel to the women who had come to the sepulcher as dawn
was breaking that heralded a new age: "Why seek ye the living
among the dead? He is not here, but is risen: remember how he
spake unto you when he was yet in Galilee" (Luke 24:5,6).

The city had done its worst. It had combined in its blasphemy
against God, and it had wrought violence on the person of His Son.
But the way of the Cross had long before been the choice of Christ
and the will of the Father. In His discourse on the Good Shepherd
Jesus had said, "I lay down my life for the sheep. . . . Therefore doth
my Father love me because I lay down my life. . . . No man taketh it
from me, but I lay it down of myself. I have power to lay it down, and
I have power to take it again" (John 10:15,17,18).

Since eternity Christ had known what men would do to Him
and that they would do it in Jerusalem. From the merely human
point of view it is hard to imagine the Crucifixion taking place in
Galilee, perhaps within sight of the lake, or on the gently sloping
hillside where He once "opened his mouth and taught them saying . . . Blessed are the merciful: for they shall obtain mercy"
(Matt. 5:2,7). But in the fortress-city, high on the stark Judean
hills, there was always a tenseness and a fury waiting to erupt.
Here anything was possible. This is why, perhaps, we can under-

stand a little better what happened that day on Golgotha.

It was the culmination, we know now, of centuries of experimentation in the history of mankind. It had all begun in another garden in which man had been meant to live forever, but where things had gone wrong. Subjected to a simple test, he had failed. Henceforth he would till a cursed earth and eat bread by the sweat of his brow. And he would die. Adam was told this in Eden, and he had to leave a perfect paradise.

But already the way back had been planned. For in that same garden Satan had been told that the seed of the woman would one day "bruise his head" (Gen. 3:15). A "peculiar" people would follow a tent across the sandy wastes and through the wilderness and worship an unseen God in the midst of their tabernacle. They would offer the blood of oxen and sheep, and goats and pigeons, as atonement for their sins, and they would commemorate by a special Passover sacrifice their escape from the plague that slew all the firstborn in Egypt. They would possess a city and build a temple, and from their royal line of kings would come the Redeemer promised four thousand years before in Eden. Their whole Mosaic ritual would be a perfect foreshadowing of the Christ in His person and work. And in the fullness of time the Messiah came, but "his own received him not" (John 1:11), and by their rejection salvation came to the Gentiles — something we can understand no more than we can the mystery of the Incarnation or the mystery of God Himself.

At the end the road had led up from Jericho to a city poised to strike and set too for its own destruction, to the crown of thorns, and then out beyond the walls to Golgotha. Man was to have his way, but it would be in accordance with the whole progressive plan of redemption. For when the earth trembled and the rocks split, the veil of the temple, blue and purple and scarlet and made of fine twined linen covered with cherubim, was torn in two, signifying the death of the Lord of the sanctuary and setting aside the entire Jewish system of worship and sacrifice.

The veil had separated the Holy Place from the "Holiest," the most sacred spot on earth into which only the high priest was permitted to enter once a year — on the Day of Atonement — with bowed head and unsandaled feet. It was a complete cube — fifteen feet in length, width, and height — lit neither by the sun nor any artificial light and filled only with the divine radiance. Before the Babylonian exile, there had stood in this innermost chamber the ark

The Spring of Gihon was before everything that is and has been Jerusalem. The mystery of old Jerusalem is reflected in its waters—the conquering of the Jebusite stronghold, the anointing of King Solomon, and the beginning of Hezekiah's Tunnel.

This pavement, named Lithostrotos in Greek, may have been the scene for the public trial of Jesus. Discovered in 1931, it is the actual courtyard of the Antonia, where Jesus was condemned to death.

A garden tomb hewn out of rock and perhaps like the one where Jesus was laid. The actual tomb of Jesus was supposedly isolated by Queen Helena but was destroyed by Khalif Haken in A.D. 1009.

The Dome of the Rock, over the sacred stone of the temple, was built at the end of the seventh century by Caliph Abd el Malik Ben Merwan. A rectangular octagon, the mosque measures 63 feet on each side with a diameter of 180 feet. The dome, made of aluminum bronze, rises to a height of 108 feet and has a 78-foot diameter.

NW *From southwest corner.*

The Old City with Mount Zion and Dormition Abbey in the foreground.

The Dome of the Rock and its esplanade to the left with ancient wall in foreground.

SW *From northeast corner.*

Jewish quarter in foreground with Western Wall and Temple Mount at top left.

Mount of Olives and Garden of Gethsemane in foreground with Intercontinental Hotel at top left.

A man praying at the Wailing Wall, the western supporting wall of the Temple Mount. Now a national shrine, this hewn-stone wall survived the destruction of Jerusalem in A.D. 70 and the many other wars in the Holy City through the centuries.

The Wailing Wall, with some stones weighing over 100 tons, has become a center for mourning over the plight of the Jews. A hallowed spot in Jewish religious and national consciousness, the wall was liberated on 7 June 1967; one-quarter of a million Jews swarmed the grounds on the first day of the Feast of the Pentecost.

The Shrine of the Book, symbolizing a cave, is a subterranean build-
ing with a tunnel-shaped interior. It houses the famous Dead Sea
Scrolls, scrolls found at Masada, the Bar Khochba letters, and objects
associated with the site of discovery. Its interior induces the feeling of
being in a cave. The scroll of Isaiah, 24 feet long, is displayed upon a
platform which resembles a jar-shaped fountain.

of shittim wood, overlaid by the mercy seat of pure gold and containing the unbroken tables of the Law, a golden pot of manna, Aaron's rod that had budded, and the five books of Moses. This was the throne of God in Israel standing within His dwelling place, but which had vanished when Nebuchadnezzar took Jerusalem in 586 B.C.

And now all was changed: there was a new way of entering God's presence and of obtaining His mercy, because the veil was no longer there. Reality had replaced the shadows of symbolism; the sacrifice of bullocks and goats was no longer required. He who "thought it not robbery to be equal with God," and was so from the beginning, "humbled himself and became obedient unto death, even the death of the cross" (Phil. 2:6-8). The Jews had prosecuted, Pilate had judged, but it was the evil in all men that made the walk to betrayal in Gethsemane and the shame and the anguish of Golgotha necessary. It had to be like this. All had to be given and all endured so that what was imperfect might again become perfect. In the world's darkest hour God's gift of His Son broke the power of darkness and of death and the grave forever.

In vain the priests had set a watch to secure the tomb, and then bribed the soldiers to say the body had been stolen while they slept. Nothing could now prevent the truth from becoming known. Even the disciples at first did not believe, because they had not understood the meaning of those words: "Destroy this temple, and in three days I will raise it up" (John 2:19). Mary Magdalene thought her Lord had been laid elsewhere. But when He spoke to her in the garden she knew what had happened and so did John, that "other disciple" who came first to the sepulcher when he found the linen clothes lying neatly folded in the empty tomb (John 20:4). Proof of the Resurrection was mounting.

That same evening in the room from which He had set out for Gethsemane Jesus appeared in the midst of the ten and "showed unto them his hands and his side. . . . Then were the disciples glad when they saw the Lord" (John 20:20). It was at the dispelling of the skepticism of Thomas a week later in the same upper room that those words that were to be the basis of the new faith were spoken: "Because thou hast seen me thou hast believed: blessed are they that have not seen and yet have believed" (John 20:29). And after that it was in Galilee where He had first called Simon Peter and Andrew his brother and James and John the sons of Zebedee into His service.

The fishermen had gone back to their nets, but that night they had caught nothing. Then at daybreak they saw Jesus standing on the shore and heard Him tell them to cast out on the opposite side of the boat. When the net was full, they brought it to the edge of the water and found "a fire of coals, and fish laid thereon, and bread," and heard someone inviting them to "come and dine. . . . And none of the disciples durst ask him, Who art thou? knowing it was the Lord" (John 21:9,12).

The scene is of a nature and quality quite beyond human power to evaluate correctly. Nothing quite like it presents itself in any other part of the Bible, and its effect on the seven disciples gathered that day in a place beloved because of its memories must have been tremendous. It is abundantly clear that about the Resurrection there was to be not the faintest shadow of doubt, for Paul too, twenty-seven years later, was to write: "He was seen of Cephas [Peter], then of the twelve: after that, he was seen of above five hundred brethren at once. . . . After that, he was seen of James, then of all the apostles. And last of all he was seen of me" (1 Cor. 15:5-8). At various times and in various places — in a garden, on a country road, at the side of a lake, in an upper room — "he showed himself alive . . . by many infallible proofs," until one day "a cloud received him out of their sight," and the disciples returned "unto Jerusalem from the mount called Olivet, which is from Jerusalem a sabbath day's journey" (Acts 1:3,9,12).

Tragedy had turned to triumph; there was now hope for them and for the world. Within the lifetime of Paul, the news of what had taken place in the Jewish capital would go to the uttermost parts of the Roman Empire. The New Testament would be written and Judaism and paganism would be challenged by the new faith. For the teachings of the Nazarene would spread and take root, and for his salvation the Jew would have to believe just like the humblest Gentile.

The days of Jerusalem and the temple were now numbered and soon complete upheaval would engulf the city. Incredible changes lay in store for the site on whose desolate surface would rise the shrines of yet another faith. Violence and division and hate would lay waste the city whose very name meant "peace," and in between her devastations pilgrims would come to walk where He had walked. For great things had happened in Jerusalem, things both terrible and glorious. And for the present, there was rejoicing in an upper room. Not only had He promised them eternal life, but those disciples who had just witnessed the Ascension from above Bethany had been reminded that one day He would return.

He would return to the city that had crucified Him and was soon to disappear in flames.

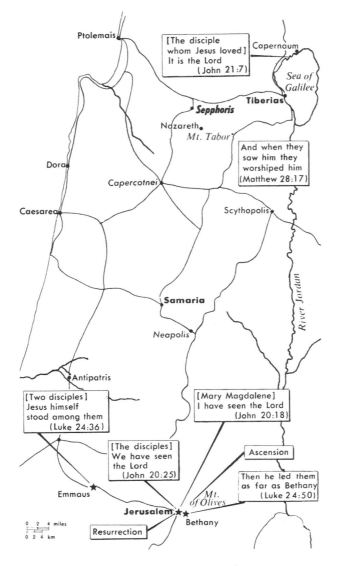

Jesus' appearances after his resurrection.

21
"Masada Shall Not Fall Again"

THERE IS AN IMMENSE irony about Jerusalem's history for the next forty years — the years between the Crucifixion and the arrival of Titus with the Roman legions before the city's walls in A.D. 70. For mankind in general, they were fateful, decisive years. In the span of one generation the seeds of Christianity were sown throughout the civilized world. It was in Jerusalem on that memorable day "when Pentecost was fully come" that the disciples went forth to establish daily autonomous congregations of new believers. But all the time the proud, enigmatical center of Judaism, still glorying in the dazzling magnificence of its temple, was drawing nearer to its predicted destruction.

For its last few remaining years Jerusalem became the scene of persecution of those won over to the new faith. The disciples ignored the commands to stop preaching and said they "ought to obey God rather than men" (Acts 5:29). They told the same Sanhedrin that had condemned Jesus that it had "denied the Holy One and the Just . . . and killed the Prince of life," but that God had exalted Him to be a Savior and that there was "none other name under heaven given among men, whereby we must be saved" (Acts 3:14,15; 4:12). Many of the Jews listened, saw the miracles that were performed, and believed. But one day an incensed Jewish hierarchy "cut to the heart" by the bold, accusing words of a young deacon of the church, cast him out of the city and stoned him.

The martyrdom of Stephen was in every way significant. It terminated a short but dynamic epoch in Christianity; it marked the introduction of one of the chief persecutors of the new faith whose "threatenings and slaughter" (Acts 9:1) resulted in the dissemina-

151

tion of the gospel far beyond the walls of Jerusalem: and it has acted as a source of inspiration down the ages to those who have suffered for their beliefs. The stoning could very well have taken place at "the place of a skull," for that is where such things were carried out. And it could easily have been through the same gate that Jesus had borne His cross four years before that the Sanhedrin, turned into an angry mob by Stephen's historic speech, now hustled the young convert.

But if the record is vague on these particular points, it is not so on others. About Stephen's last moments there is a brilliant clarity. As he died he saw "the heavens opened, and the Son of man standing on the right hand of God" (Acts 7:56). For his executioners he sought only forgiveness: "Lord, lay not this sin to their charge" (Acts 7:60). And it was these who, in order to perform their awful task, "laid down their clothes at a young man's feet whose name was Saul" (Acts 7:58).

It is difficult to imagine a stranger introduction to perhaps the greatest Christian of all time — Saul of Tarsus, son of a Pharisee, a Jew by faith, nationality, and culture, who had sat at the feet of the great Gamaliel and had all the laws of Judaism coursing through his veins. This was the Saul who was to make havoc of the church and drive it behind locked doors in Jerusalem. Persecution under him was to reach new heights, until those he hunted fled to Samaria and beyond. But this was also the Saul who was to become a changed person on the road to Damascus, who was soon to wear the mantle of the man to whose death he was now consenting, and who, thirty years later, was to die for the same faith. This was the tentmaker, who was to take the gospel to Cyprus and Macedonia, to Athens and Ephesus and Corinth, and finally to Rome. In missionary journeys covering over six thousand miles he was to suffer shipwreck, stripes, and imprisonment, and one day, because he was a Roman citizen, he would appeal to Caesar for justice. At the stoning of Stephen the light of the infant church seemed almost to go out. But standing by that day, watching, was a man of purest Jewish blood who was to become the great apostle to the Gentiles.

But as the new faith spread in all directions, the shadows lengthened over the Old City and the temple mount. Christ had come and gone. The road from Bethlehem to Golgotha had crossed the city many times and had ended in triumph at the empty tomb. The disciples continued to meet in the outer precincts of the temple, for it was at the Beautiful Gate that Peter and John performed their first miracle when they healed the lame man there at the hour of prayer. It was from the temple that Paul, in the act of fulfilling a vow, was dragged by his enemies and had to be rescued by Roman soldiers. For him the road led eventually to Rome and decapitation under Nero somewhere, it is believed, along the Ostian Way. Forsaken at the end by all except Luke, he must always have taken courage from those words of the Lord: "Be of good cheer, Paul; for as thou hast testified of me in Jerusalem, so must thou bear witness also at Rome" (Acts 23:11). Paul had borne witness at Rome. He had "fought a good fight and kept the faith." Two years after a fire had destroyed a greater part of Rome and Nero had used Christians as human torches in his palace gardens, Paul's valiant, tempestuous life came to an end. It was A.D. 66 — the year the Jews rose against their masters in far-off Palestine.

It took the Roman Empire seven years to subdue the little strip of land that lies like a narrow bridge between Asia and Africa. Nothing quite like the mixture of heroism and insanity that marked the defense of Jerusalem midway through that confrontation has ever been seen since. And nobody who visits Israel today leaves without visiting the mountain fortress overlooking the Dead Sea where the seven-year struggle began — and where it ended. Today the site of the last encounter where 960 Jews committed suicide rather than fall into the hands of the enemy has become a shrine and a symbol to the nation. When the young Israeli graduates at his military academy, he swears an oath: "Masada shall not fall again." What he has vowed to hold today, of course, is more than an isolated rock mass soaring over a slowly shrinking salt lake in the Judean wilderness. It is a country he ceased to rule, in the full sense of the word, 2,500 years ago, but which he rules again, conscious only in part of the trust committed to him.

As the first century of the Christian era advanced, the lot of the Jews grew more desperate. It was, indeed, one of the worst of times for this unhappy people. Their governors had been getting steadily more brutal and more corrupt and with the advent of Gessius Florus, breaking point was reached. At least Albinus, whom Florus succeeded, "did the greater part of his rogueries in private, and with a sort of dissimulation."[1] Under the latter "there were now no bounds

---

[1] This and following quotations in this chapter are taken from Josephus, *Wars of the Jews.*

to the nation's miseries, and it was he who necessitated us to take up arms against the Romans, while we thought it better to be destroyed at once, than little by little." If it was, as the Jewish historian Josephus contends, Florus's "design to have a war kindled," it was a decision of the Jews themselves that seemingly made hostilities on a large scale inevitable. And in perfect keeping with the irony that has marked so much of this history, the spark that ignited the blaze that was eventually to consume the temple originated in this quarter. On the advice of one called Eleazer, son of Ananias the high priest, and governor of the temple, and against all counsel of the moderates, an embargo was suddenly placed on gifts or sacrifices by any foreigner. As this included Rome and the emperor for whom up to now a daily sacrifice had been offered, the die was cast.

But while the stage was being set in Jerusalem for the fearful civil strife that was to rend it within while the Romans battered its walls from without, the Jews had won their first victory. They had captured the fortress of Masada. Exactly how this was accomplished is not recorded, but in the light of subsequent events, it can only have been, as Josephus says, "by treachery," for after the fall of Jerusalem a handful of patriots were able to hold out there against a Roman army for almost a year. Masada was an understandably tempting objective. In it was a prerequisite for any insurrection: an assortment of arms sufficient to equip ten thousand men, which Manahem, leader of the successful exploit, distributed among his band before returning to Jerusalem — and his own doom.

Masada, like Jerusalem, can haunt the memory. It is part of a region that bears every proof of having incurred divine wrath. The fire and brimstone that destroyed Sodom and Gomorrah four thousand years ago would seem to have blighted forever the surrounding landscape. Here you are at the bottom of the world, 1,300 feet below sea level, in a valley of desolation where the crags and mountains rear up from the shore of the vast lake in weird and tortuous shapes, their barren slopes split by deep, empty ravines. A sort of fog hangs over the motionless stretch of water, 50 miles long, 10 miles wide, and, at its northern end, some 1,200 feet deep. Through this lunarlike wilderness the tarred road twists its way to industrial plants and the other creations of man that are utterly incongruous here. Even the few oases seem a gross intrusion in this land of Sodom. For the Dead Sea — the Arabs call it "the Sea of Lot," and the Romans knew it as Lake Asphaltitis — is also a source of life.

From its salty waters today various bromides, potash, fertilizers, fumigating materials, and other chemicals are being extracted in ever-increasing quantities. Even in Josephus's day it had its use, for "in many parts of it," he says, "black clods of bitumen were cast up which swam at the top of the water, and resemble both in shape and bigness headless bulls. . . . This bitumen is not only useful for the caulking of ships, but for the cure of men's bodies; accordingly it is mixed in a great many medicines."

And it was in this strange world of desolation in 37 B.C. that Herod, who built the temple, who sought the life of the infant Jesus, who was buried with such pomp in the fortress tomb at Herodium, also sought a refuge from two kinds of danger. The first was a fear of being deposed by the Jews, the second, "greater and more terrible," was that Cleopatra, Queen of Egypt, might wish to add Judea to her empire. "So the fear of these made Herod rebuild Masada, and thereby leave it for the finishing stroke of the Romans in the Jewish War." Only his megalomaniacal genius could have planned what has lain hidden on the summit of this natural fastness for nearly two thousand years.

On its fairly level summit half a mile long and 220 yards wide was built a winter palace, huge storehouses, and an enormous reservoir. At the northern end of the plateau another palace was constructed on three levels, with Corinthian columns and mosaic floors; and the whole area was surrounded by an eighteen-foot wall with thirty-eight towers. It was the weapons placed there by Herod that fell into the hands of the Jews a hundred years later, and it was in the palaces built for him that the bodies of the last defenders of this fortress were found by the Roman legions under Flavius Silva on 15 April, A.D. 73.

Modern engineering has made the conquest of Masada easy. You can drive to the base by car from Jerusalem in a few hours and reach the top by cable car in less than five minutes. But for ten thousand legionnaires and auxiliary forces, carrying siege equipment of the first century through this mountainous wasteland must have been something of a nightmare. Remains of their camps, a three-mile wall encircling the entire fortress, and a massive earthen ramp on the landward side from which the final assault was launched, are still there, as are many other reminders of one of the strangest dramas in history. The secrets of Masada have been kept through the centuries because it stands in all its stark majesty in the heart of the Judean desert. And the most precious of Professor Yigael Yadin's discoveries there in the 1960s were parchments of Scripture corresponding word for word with the Masoretic text.

Not everyone in the historic suicide pact in 73 died. When the Romans advanced over the summit to join battle with the besieged, they were met only by "a terrible solitude on every side and a fire within the palace." After a while "an ancient woman, and another who was kin to Eleazar [the leader of the defenders] and superior to most women in prudence and learning," and five children emerged from an underground cavern. The second of these women, says Josephus, "clearly described all that was said and done, and the manner of it." Even, it seems, providing a remarkable synopsis of Eleazar ben Yair's exhortations and philosophical discourse before the 960 perished by their own free will. It was infinitely better to leave this world in a state of freedom, than to become slaves to an enemy, better to leave an example that would both astonish him and win his admiration. And perhaps playing his trump card, Eleazar had reminded his hearers of "the city that was believed to have God himself inhabiting it. 'Where,' he asked, 'is now the great metropolis of the Jewish nation, fortified by so many walls, containing so many instruments prepared for war, and thousands of men to fight for it? It is now demolished to the very foundations with some unfortunate old men lying upon the ashes of the temple, and a few women preserved there alive by the enemy for our bitter shame and reproach. . . . I cannot but wish that we had all died before we had seen the holy city so profanely treated.' "

This was the simple though unpalatable truth. For nearly three years Jerusalem had been nothing more than a Roman camp. With the fall of Masada, a nation's brave but unavailing resistance came to an end. It seemed the Jew was already beginning to reap the bitter fruit of those terrible words "His blood be on our heads." But though his citadels were falling one by one, the Jew would survive, and one day he would return both to Masada and to Jerusalem when the power of those who had now conquered them was only a memory.

PART III
The Final Dawn

And I will rejoice in Jerusalem, and joy in my people: and the voice of weeping shall be no more heard in her, nor the voice of crying. . . . And it shall come to pass, that every one that is left of all the nations which came against Jerusalem shall even go up from year to year to worship the King, the Lord of hosts, and to keep the feast of tabernacles. — Isaiah 65:19; Zechariah 14:16

22
War Against Rome

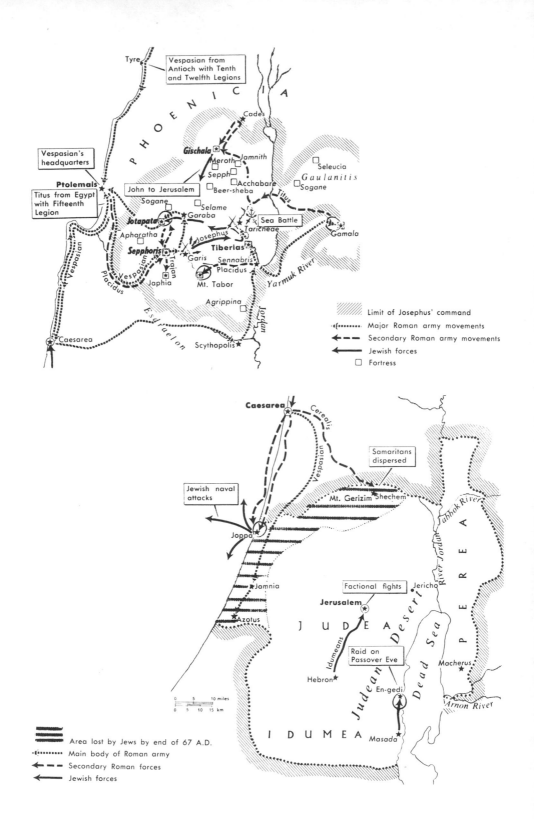

Tyre

P H O E N I C I A

Cades

Gischala

Jamnith

Meroth

Sepph

Seleucia

Gaulanitis

Acchabare

Sogane

Beer-sheba

Titus

Vespasian's headquarters

John to Jerusalem

Ptolemais

Sogane

Titus from Egypt with Fifteenth Legion

Selame

Goraba

Jotapata

Apharatha

Josephus

Sea Battle

Tarichaee

Gamala

Sepphoris

Tiberias

Garis

Sennabris

Vespasian

Trajan

Placidus

Japhia

Mt. Tabor

Placidus

Yarmuk River

Esdraelon

Agrippina

Jordan

Limit of Josephus' command

Major Roman army movements

Secondary Roman army movements

Jewish forces

Fortress

Caesarea

Scythopolis

Caesarea

Cerealis

Samaritans dispersed

Jewish naval attacks

Mt. Gerizim

Shechem

Jabbok River

Vespasian

Joppa

P E R E A

River Jordan

Jamnia

Factional fights

Jerusalem

Jericho

Azotus

J U D E A

Judean Desert

Dead Sea

Idumeans

Raid on Passover Eve

Hebron

En-gedi

Macherus

0   5   10 miles

0   5   10 15 km

I D U M E A

Masada

Arnon River

Area lost by Jews by end of 67 A.D.

Main body of Roman army

Secondary Roman forces

Jewish forces

BETWEEN THE CAPTURE of Masada by a band of Zealots and its repossession by the Romans seven years later lay an ocean of blood and the shattered hopes of an indestructible people. Forty years after it had been predicted, the storm had broken with savage fury over the length and breadth of the land and laid waste its capital. In the hills of Samaria and in the byways of Galilee where Jesus had walked with His disciples and extolled the blessedness of the peacemakers, men perished in their thousands by the sword and the engines of war. One by one the Jewish strongholds were reduced to smoking ruins, the armor-clad Roman legions at times showing no mercy whatsoever. Even the lake that once was ordered to be still became, one day during the battle for Taricheae, "all bloody and full of dead bodies, with not one of the Jews escaping from the sea-fight." Galilee, in fact, "was all over filled with fire and blood," before the enemy finally dealt with the country's metropolis. Disaster had once again overtaken "a peculiar people."

While Manahem was busy plundering the armory of Herod on top of Masada, the tension in Jerusalem had come to a head with continuing provocative action by Florus, the procurator. At his instigation, a deputation led by temple dignitaries that had gone out to meet two cohorts of reinforcements from Caesarea were senselessly attacked. Florus, it seems, also had designs on the temple treasures and in the ensuing panic his forces attempted to storm Antonia. The cloisters linking the fortress with the temple, however, were wrecked by the Jews and the bid failed. Florus retired to Caesarea, and the Jews, now at explosion point, turned to King Agrippa for help. This was the Agrippa who, listening to Paul's defense a few

161

years before, had told the apostle, "Almost thou persuadest me to be a Christian" (Acts 26:28).

Agrippa's impassioned and cleverly reasoned speech, climaxed by the claim that divine assistance was already on the side of "the vast Roman Empire," met with initial success. But his plea that Florus should be obeyed until "Caesar should send one to succeed him" incensed the extremists who "had the impudence to throw stones at him." An angry Agrippa retired to his own kingdom, and a city began its long night of terror. It was August, 66. For the next four years Jerusalem was to know no peace as Jew fought Jew or Roman within and without her walls, and famine in the end "devoured the people by whole houses and families."

Soon after Agrippa's departure, Eleazar placed his embargo on the temple sacrifice for Caesar and the moderates, in a last bid to avert open war, again appealed to Agrippa who sent three thousand cavalry to their aid. With these the priests, and those still desirous of peace, seized the upper city (Mount Zion) while the more rebellious moved into the lower city and the temple under Eleazar. After a week's fighting, the Romans were driven from the upper city, the Antonia was taken, and its garrison slaughtered. The Caesarean cohort then took refuge in Herod's palace with its three great towers — Hippicus, Mariamne, and Phasael — and it was at this point that Manahem returned from Masada, became leader of the rebel forces, and continued operations against the enemy in the palace.

Spurning an offer of capitulation from those in the palace, Manahem forced them to flee into the towers and killed those who did not reach their safety. The following day he disposed of Ananias the high priest, and also his brother. But his increasing pomposity and tyranny was not all that well received and he soon came to a violent end at the hands of the general populace. His place was taken by Eleazar who promptly revealed a character every bit as cruel and as treacherous as that of the man he had helped to eliminate. After being promised their liberty if they surrendered, those trapped in the three towers were promptly murdered after they had laid down their arms. Only their general, Metilius, saved his life by promising to convert to Judaism. "This loss to the Romans," says Josephus, "was but light . . . but still it appeared to be a prelude to the Jews' own destruction . . . so the city was filled with sadness, and every one of the moderate men in it were under great disturbance, for indeed it so happened that this murder was perpetrated on the sabbath day, on which day the Jews have respite from their works on account of Divine worship."

It was certainly a day for misgivings in Jerusalem. Not only had the specter of civil strife raised its ugly head; the war against Rome had also begun. And proof of this was not long in coming. When news of the massacre of the cohort got through to Caesarea where Florus had his headquarters, 20,000 Jews perished in an hour. Their kith and kin retaliated by attacking cities throughout Palestine, and at last the dilatory Cestius Gallus, legate of Syria, was compelled to act. Marching south at the head of some 30,000 troops he had Joppa burnt, and over 8,000 of its inhabitants killed. He succeeded in subduing Galilee and the coast and then set off for Jerusalem. He dallied for three days on "the elevation called Scopus" before setting an area called Bezetha (or the New City) on fire. An assault on the northern portion of the temple failed but just when the moderates were about to hand over the city, "Cestius retired without any reason in the world." Encouraged by this unexpected withdrawal, the Jews set off in pursuit and only night saved the Roman army. As it was, Cestius was forced to abandon a great quantity of equipment including his siege engines and lost 5,300 footmen and 380 horsemen. "Running and singing," the Jews returned to their metropolis, ignorant of the far greater ordeal that lay ahead. It was the end of October and the twelfth year of Nero's reign.

With hostilities on a large scale now unavoidable, a council-of-war was held in the temple at which generals and administrators for other parts of the country were appointed. Among these were thirty-year-old Flavius Josephus himself, son of Matthias, who was given the governorship of both Galilees and of Gamala "the strongest city in those parts," and who set about "building walls in proper places about Jotapata, Bersabee, and Selamis . . . and Taricheae and Tiberius. He also got together an army out of Galilee, of more than 100,000 young men, all of which he armed with old weapons which he had collected together and prepared for them." But for the next few months Josephus had not only the Romans to contend with but also the bandits of a treacherous individual known as John of Gischala, who was to become one of the leading figures in the closing stages of the Jerusalem drama.

It was not, however, until the middle of the following year, 67, that Josephus's remarkable versatility was put to perhaps its greatest test — at the battle for Jotapata. At this key engagement of the

Galilean campaign, he came face to face with the only man whom
Nero, in February of that year, had decided was capable of bearing
"the great burden of so mighty a war" — Titus Flavius Vespasian.
Born of humble parentage, Vespasian was, from all accounts, both
honorable and able, had commanded a legion in Germany and
Britain and had "from his youth been exercised in warlike exploits."
Now 58, this was the Roman who was to redden the lake of Galilee
with Jewish blood, subdue the rest of Palestine, and then leave the
conquest of Jerusalem to his son Titus while he went to Rome to
become emperor and the tenth of the twelve Caesars.

Jotapata was a formidable stronghold "almost all of it being built
on a precipice" and rather like Jerusalem, vulnerable only to the
north. It had already survived one Roman assault before Vespasian
turned his attention to it. For forty-seven days siege engines hurled
stones, darts, and javelins onto the city while battering rams, "vast
beams of wood like the masts of ships, with thick pieces of iron at the
forepart," pounded away at the walls. In the end, treachery played a
part in the city's capture. On the same day that the banks set up by
the Romans became higher than the walls, a deserter let it be known
that the last watch was in the habit of falling asleep. Acting on this
information, Vespasian soon had the city in his hands. Forty
thousand defenders were slain, but Josephus, their commander, was
not among them. With some forty others he eluded capture for a few
days, and survived at the same time, "either by chance or the
providence of God," a suicide pact with his companions.

Brought eventually before his conqueror, he said that he came
"as a messenger with great tidings. 'Thou, O Vespasian art Caesar
and Emperor, thou and thy son [Titus had also taken part in the
siege] with thee." This was not unpleasant news and though skepti-
cal at first, Vespasian was not long in accepting the prophecy as
possibly a true one. With it Josephus saved his life, but his military
activities were now over. He was held prisoner until Vespasian,
"remembering his valiant defence of Jotapata and regretting he had
been so long in bonds, ordered his release soon after becoming
Emperor."

Systematic reduction of centers of Jewish resistance continued
for the best part of a year. Joppa was taken for the second time before
the Romans, after a three weeks' rest at Caesarea Philippi, moved
down on Tiberius and Taricheae. The former surrendered without
bloodshed, but it was in the ensuing battle for Taricheae that the lake

of Galilee was crimsoned with the slaughter of some six thousand Jews while as many were sent by Vespasian to assist Nero in cutting the Corinth Canal, and another thirty thousand were sold as slaves. On the opposite side of the lake the city of Gamala, an even more natural stronghold than Jotapata, and one also fortified by Josephus, held out for twenty-three days. Of the nine thousand inhabitants, four thousand were slain by the Romans, and five thousand threw themselves over the precipices at the fall of the city.

Fugitives from Gadora and other parts of the country made a stand on the banks of the Jordan where, in hand-to-hand fighting, fifteen thousand were slain, and "the river could be passed over by reason of the dead bodies." With the occupation of the small city of Gischala, farther north, the first phase of the war was over. It was from this city that John, "a cunning knave, and of a temper that could take on various shapes," fled with his band of ruffians who were to terrorize Jerusalem. "And thus was all Galilee taken, but this not until after it had cost the Romans much pain."

And now, waiting its turn, stood the royal city high on the Judean hills, rapidly becoming a haven for all and sundry. Toward it Vespasian set his course, but he was not destined to add the conquest of Jerusalem to his list of triumphs. For on 9 June, 68, he received the news that Nero, to escape execution, had died by his own hand. The war in Palestine came to a halt, and for the next eighteen months the Empire was more than occupied by its disorders as three emperors followed one another in quick succession. Galba (73) ruled for seven months until January of 69 when he was slain in "the midst of the market place in Rome." He was succeeded by Otho (37) who committed suicide after being in power for three months. His forces had been defeated by Aulus Vitellius, who in turn was crushed at a battle near Cremona by the legions that had now come out in support of Vespasian. Vitellius was killed in Rome, and by the end of October 69, Vespasian was at the head of the Empire. Although he had for some time been accepted by Alexandria and the East as emperor, it was not until the following October that he reached Rome. Except for isolated fortresses, all Judea and Idumaea had then been overrun by the Romans, and Titus, elder son of the new ruler of the Empire, after a four-and-a-half-months' siege, was master of Jerusalem.

All quotations are from Josephus, *Wars of the Jews.*

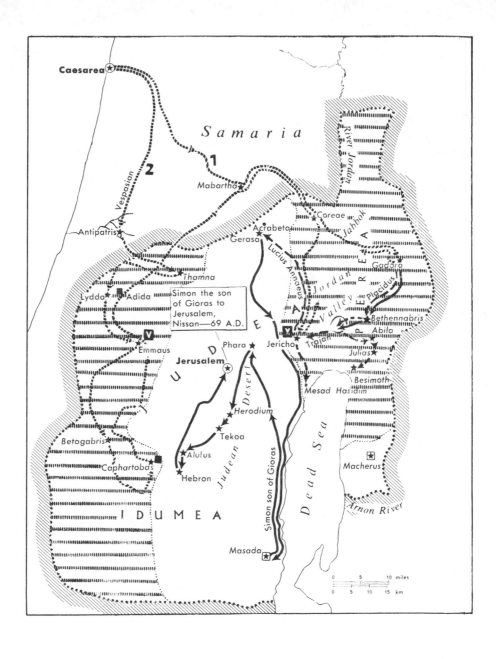

Caesarea

Samaria

2 Vespasian **1**

Mabartha

Antipatris

Coreae

Acrabeta

Gerasa

River Jordan

Lucius Annaeus

Jabbok

Thamna

Lydda Adida

Simon the son
of Gioras to
Jerusalem,
Nissan—69 A.D.

Gadora

Bethennabris

Abila

Emmaus

Phara

Jericho

Julias

Trajan Placidus

Jerusalem

Herodium

Tekoa

Besimoth

Mesad Hasidim

Betogabris

Alulus

Caphartobas

Hebron

Simon son of Gioras

Judean Desert

Jordan Valley

P E R E A

J U D E A

I D U M E A

Macherus

Dead Sea

Masada

Arnon River

| 0 | 5 | 10 miles |

| 0 | 5 | 10 | 15 | km |

V	Garrisoning legion and its number
■	Roman garrison
←	Jewish forces
◄.......	Main Roman army

◄ – –'	Secondary Roman army movements
....	Border of area of Revolt—start of 68 A.D.
....	Border of area of Revolt—end of 68 A.D.
▦▦▦	Area lost by Jews during 68 A.D.

Vespasian's campaign in A.D. *68.*

23
Triumph of Titus

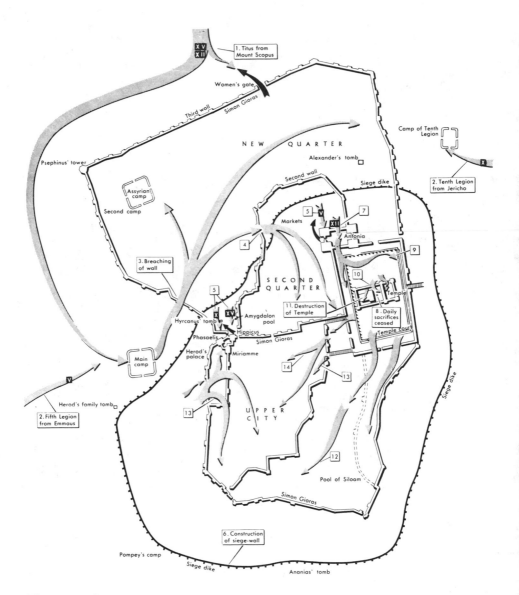

1. Titus from Mount Scopus

Women's gate

Third wall

Simon Gioras

Camp of Tenth Legion

2. Tenth Legion from Jericho

Psephinus' tower

N E W   Q U A R T E R

Alexander's tomb

Assyrian camp

Second camp

Second wall

Siege dike

Markets

5

7

Antonia

9

3. Breaching of wall

4

S E C O N D
Q U A R T E R

10

Temple

5

X

XV

Amygdalon pool

11. Destruction of Temple

8. Daily sacrifices ceased

Hyrcanus' tomb

Phasaelis

Hippicus

Simon Gioras

Temple Court

Herod's palace

Miriamme

14

13

Main camp

13

U P P E R

C I T Y

V

Herod's family tomb

2. Fifth Legion from Emmaus

12

Pool of Siloam

Siege dike

Simon Gioras

6. Construction of siege-wall

Pompey's camp

Siege dike

Ananias' tomb

The siege of Jerusalem in A.D. 70.

Titus came, he saw, and he conquered; Judea and its eternal city was left as a woman, bound and weeping, sitting beneath a palm tree.

O N MAY 10, A.D. 70, the shadow of Titus fell across the walls of Jerusalem. To this handsome, thirty-year-old Roman, already a veteran in the art of war, had fallen the hardest task of the now four-year-old war — capture of the Jewish capital. It had already had two reprieves. Cestius Gallus withdrew suddenly in October of 67 when the city was his for the taking. Nero's death had stopped Vespasian's march on it nine months later. But there were to be no more reprieves. This time the enemy from outside the gate and the enemy within were each to contribute to its utter destruction. It took Titus's army of 65,000 men 139 days to gain control of the whole city and during that time, if we accept Josephus's account as authentic, it was spared no variety of savagery or horror.

It is not surprising that forty years before, He who knew what lay ahead had told those in Jerusalem who were sorrowing on His behalf to "weep for themselves and their children" (Luke 23:28). The words might even have been recalled by some within the besieged walls. But tears were of no use now. The time had come when *"a deep silence and a kind of deadly night had seized upon the city."* Those who were not dying at the hands of rival factions were starving to death in their thousands. Titus had thrown a wall around the whole city to prevent anyone from escaping. The time had come when "girdles and shoes and the very leather from shields was chewed upon, when children and young men wandered about the marketplace like shadows, some even searching the common sewers and old dunghills of cattle for something to eat, when terrible methods of torment were invented by robbers to discover where food was hidden . . . and everyone died with his eyes fixed upon the Temple."

Jerusalem had arrived at that time in her history when decent burials no longer took place and the dead were cast down from the walls into the valleys below. Fugitives and deserters who fell into the hands of those beyond the walls were dissected for gold or any money they might have hidden within their beings. Hunger had begun to unhinge people's minds to the extent that nothing too terrible was ruled out in the bid for sustenance. Even the country within a twelve-mile radius took on a naked look as the trees were cut down for the construction of banks and more gruesome purposes. At one time five hundred Jews were crucified daily within sight of those on the walls, until "there was no more room to erect crosses and no more wood could be found for bodies." Perhaps, as the defenders gazed at this harrowing sight, some may have remembered that other cross at the foot of which the Roman soldiers cast lots for a coat that was "without seam" (John 19:23).

But before Titus arrived at Jerusalem with the fifth, tenth, twelfth, and fifteenth legions and a host of auxiliaries, "the state of the city was already that of a place doomed to destruction." No contention of Josephus is so well supported, though admittedly by himself, as this. He is in no doubt as to what lay at the root of the catastrophe that overtook his people in the Holy City. "Sedition destroyed the city," he says, "and the Romans destroyed the sedition, which it was a much harder thing to do than to destroy the walls; so that we may justly ascribe our misfortunes to our own people, and the just vengeance taken on them to the Romans . . . for this internal sedition did not cease even when the Romans were encamped near their very walls. But although they had grown wiser at the first onset the Romans made upon them, this lasted but a while; for they returned to their former madness, and separated one from another, and fought it out and did everything that the besiegers could desire them to do; for they never suffered anything that was worse from the Romans than they made each other suffer. . . ." Whether indeed Titus would have taken Jerusalem had he not found the city divided against itself will never be known. But it had to fall — sometime — so that not one stone of its temple was left upon another.

When John of Gischala arrived in the city with his band of fugitives, it was already harboring many who "omitted no kind of barbarity" and who had turned "the sanctuary into a refuge and shop of tyranny." Against these the high priest Ananus had rallied the law-abiding citizens and there had been several armed clashes. The lie was then spread that Roman aid was to be sought and John of Gischala persuaded his desperadoes to follow suit by calling in the Idumeans "naturally a most barbarous and bloody nation." Before long, twenty thousand of these, put into battle array under four commanders, were at the gates of Jerusalem, which they found shut against them, and a deputy high priest boldly asking why "had they come to protect a sink of wicked wretches, the offscouring of the whole country, and each one deserving ten thousand deaths?"

His words fell on deaf ears, the rage of the newcomers merely increasing the longer they were kept outside the city. That night at the height of a storm the Zealots succeeded in sawing through the bars of one of the gates and admitted their allies. *The result was a reign of terror* which saw Ananus and twenty thousand like-minded moderates summarily dispatched, the outer courts of the temple overflowing with blood, and those who survived envious of those who now had nothing more to fear. In a word, it was a time when "no other gentle passion was so entirely lost, as mercy." And following the course of events from a distance was Vespasian, curbing his commanders' impatience to march on Jerusalem, with the observation that "while their enemies were destroying one another with their own hands it was best to sit still as spectators." Then, as suddenly as they had appeared, the Idumeans left the city, but not before they had released twenty thousand people from custody, who immediately set off to join another adventurer who was to write his name in blood on the pavements and streets of Jerusalem — Simon Bar Giora.

Simon Bar Giora began life in Gerasa (Jerash), one of the cities of the Decapolis, and had led a successful attack on the rear forces of Cestius Gallus at the start of the war, at Bethoron. Incurring the displeasure of Ananus, the high priest, he had cast in his lot for a time with those who had seized Masada and proceeded with them on several expeditions of pillage and plunder in the vicinity of the mountain fortress. He then set out on his own, "proclaiming liberty to all those in slavery, and getting together a set of wicked men from all quarters." As he ventured farther afield, his conquests multiplied and his power grew until "his army was no longer composed of slaves and robbers but a great many of the populace were obedient unto him as their king." Idumea suffered the worst at the hands of his marauding army, now grown to forty thousand.

One day, in pursuit of his enemies, Simon arrived at the walls of Jerusalem. The Romans themselves, says Josephus, could not have struck more terror into the hearts of those within, who now had two tyrants to contend with, plus the prospect of a long-delayed assault by a common foe. The activities of the Zealots under John had reached a stage where the whole safety of the city was in jeopardy. So, driven to a "remedy that was to prove worse than the disease," Matthias, the high priest, went out to seek the aid of Simon who "in an arrogant manner granted them his lordly protection and came into the city in order to deliver it from the Zealots." It was the third year of the war and Jerusalem had taken another step toward the abyss. Vespasian had brought all but the fortresses of Herodium, Masada, and Macherus under his control and, assured of support from the eastern part of the Empire, was about to take over from Vitellius. It was time for him to go west to Italy and for his son to bring to a conclusion the affairs in Judea.

The last round in the protracted struggle was about to start and as Titus marched his troops northward from Alexandria in Egypt through the desert and on to Gaza, Ashkelon, Jamnia, and Joppa, and then to Caesarea, the sedition in Jerusalem had taken on the form of a "wild beast grown mad." Three factions were now engaged in trying to eliminate one another, while among them the main populace was like "a great body torn in pieces," and the aged had even begun to look for the Romans to come and deliver them from their misery. The city had been divided into three sectors, with Eleazar (who had begun all the trouble) ensconced in the inner court of the temple with some two thousand Zealots, John of Gischala with six thousand armed men below him in the outer courts, and Simon Bar Giora in the upper city with ten thousand under his command and a further five thousand Idumeans as allies. The three agreed at this stage in nothing but "to kill those that were innocent, the temple was defiled everywhere with murders," and John and Simon then succeeded in destroying by fire reserves of corn and other provisions that would have kept the city from starving for years.

Such was the state of Jerusalem when one day in the spring of A.D. 70 the Romans arrived. For nearly five months they were denied total victory, the common danger at last serving to unite those within the city. Titus pitched his first camp about four miles from the walls, and almost lost his life when he and six hundred horsemen were ambushed on a reconnaissance of the city outskirts. The following day the legions moved up, with the tenth occupying the Mount of Olives. Loath to see the Romans fortify this position unhindered, the Jews sallied forth and fell on them "with great eagerness and a prodigious shout." Only the intervention and bravery of Titus himself saved the legion from a humiliating defeat. The struggle for Jerusalem had begun — at the very place where its destruction had been prophesied forty years previously. It was to become more bitter and more bloody by the day as the fanaticism of a section of the besieged increased with every new calamity.

With the help of battering rams, banks, seventy-five-foot towers, and machines that hurled immense stones, darts, and javelins nearly five hundred yards, the Romans gained possession of the two outer walls of the city after twenty-five days and then came up against even more formidable obstacles in the shape of the Antonia fortress and beyond it the sanctuary itself — "for the Temple was a fortress that guarded the city, as was the tower of Antonia a guard to the Temple." The Jews had contested every inch of ground, undermining the Roman banks, setting fire to their machines, and engaging in bitter hand-to-hand fighting.

Although a four-day parade of the entire enemy forces in all their dazzling war equipment awed the defenders, it brought no petitions for peace; nor did a highly emotional plea by Josephus, sent by Titus to speak to the Jews in their own language. Finding a place that was "out of reach of their darts and yet within their hearing," the former Rabbi and one-time commander of their forces in Galilee, said they must surely know the Roman powers were invincible, that "fortune on all hands had gone over to them, and in fact God had now settled in Italy." Wisdom lay in changing their conduct before their calamities became incurable, for there was no sense in leaving the "city empty of inhabitants and the country a desert; on which account Caesar did now offer them his right hand for their security."

When the net result of this was a shower of darts and scornful reproach, Josephus tried another avenue of approach. He ranged over Hebrew history. When did the Jews, he asked, ever conquer other nations by their own hands and their own weapons? When did God, Creator of the Jewish people, not avenge them when they had been injured? Was it not time they considered how great a Supporter they had profanely abused? It was not only against the Romans that they were fighting, but against God Himself. Did not God bring them out of Egypt, slay the army of Sennacherib, and restore this temple and city to them under Cyrus? But they could hardly expect divine favor when they were vying now with one another in wickedness. When the King of Babylon had burned the temple, the Jews were not as impious as they were now. God had fled from His sanctuary and stood now on the side of those against whom they were fighting. Josephus ended this mixture of reproof and supplication by offering his own life if his hearers "would but return to a sane mind after his death."

One effect of this oration was to induce some to desert to the Romans, but it also provided John and Simon with an excuse for tightening up security measures, if that indeed were possible. Hunger was also driving the poor to seek food beyond the walls, but the sight of daily crucifixions as they were caught merely elicited from the extremists the reply that they would "do all the mischief to the Romans they could while they had breath in them." Nor was the threat an idle one, for the first assault against the Antonia was stoutly repulsed. The Romans had spent seventeen days on constructing ramps on ground that John had ingeniously undermined. At the moment of attack the supporting cross-beams were set alight, the entire bank collapsed, "and many indeed despaired of taking the city with the usual engines of war." It was then that Titus decided to encircle the city with a five-mile wall before beginning a second attempt on the fortress. It was also at this point that "the famine widened its progress," and Titus was informed that "no fewer than 600,000 were thrown out at the gates."

The end was approaching. Four new banks were thrown up in twenty-one days against the Antonia, and this time the Romans took the fortress. It was nearly the end of July, and there still remained the temple, to which the Jews now withdrew. Following one of the bloodiest clashes of the siege, the Romans were driven back into the Antonia. During all this horror, the daily sacrifice had never ceased, but it did on 7 August, "for want of men to offer it." Realizing what this would mean to the Jews, Titus offered to continue the struggle elsewhere, so that no Roman would be forced to defile the temple. John's reply was to set his artillery on the gates of the sanctuary and Titus had little option but to proceed with the engagement on sacred ground.

All but the southeast tower of the Antonia was demolished to give ready access to the temple site and work was begun on raising banks at different points around the cloisters. Losing more Roman lives than he considered was justified in these operations, Titus then gave orders to set the gates on fire. From these the fire spread to the cloisters and soon the inner temple with its Holy of Holies, now the last refuge of a frenzied band of men, stood waiting for the climax. Titus, still determined to spare the sanctuary even if the Jews decided to use it as a citadel, sent soldiers to put out the fire. While doing this, they were attacked but they drove the Jews back "as far as the holy house itself. At which time one of the soldiers, without staying for any orders, being hurried on by a certain divine fury and being lifted up by another soldier, set fire to a golden window, through which there was a passage to the rooms that were about the holy house on the north side of it . . . the fatal day had come, it was the 10th day of the month of Ab upon which it was formerly burnt by the King of Babylon."

In vain Titus tried to get his soldiers to quench the flames. No one heard his shouts or paid any attention to his signals. As the fire spread, the pile of dead around the altar grew higher and higher, and "the ground did nowhere appear visible for the bodies that lay on it . . . 10,000 of those that were caught were slain, nor was there a commiseration for any age . . . but children and old men, and profane persons and priests were all slain in the same manner." From the surrounding hills returned the echo of the crackling flames, the shouts of the Roman legions and the cries of the dying. "And thus was the holy house burnt down, without Caesar's approbation . . . 1300 years, seven months and 15 days after the laying of its first foundation by King Solomon." To the growing list of those associated with the temple mount, the Roman who, after sharing power with his father, came to rule the Empire as the eleventh Caesar had added his name. Like Pompey a century before, Titus also stood in the Holy of Holies and marveled at what he saw.

But although the sanctuary had fallen, it was another three weeks before all Jerusalem was in Roman hands. From the smoldering temple the remaining Jewish resisters fled first to the lower city, rejected another offer of clemency by Titus and put forward their own terms for surrender. The result was another sector of Jerusalem extending down as far as the pool of Siloam, being burned to the ground. There remained now only the upper city with its formidable palace built by Herod and "so steep that it could not possibly be taken without raising banks." These were duly erected, and forty thousand given their freedom before the final holocaust when "the fire of many of the houses was quenched with men's blood." Titus spared only the three towers of the palace — Hippicus, Mariamne, and Phasael — and "so much of the wall as enclosed the city on the west side to afford a camp for the tenth legion, and to show to posterity what kind of city it was and how well fortified, which the Roman valour had subdued."

John, finally emerging from a cavern, begged successfully for his life. Simon, with some followers, tried to dig an escape tunnel under the temple, but the bid for freedom failed. So, "thinking he might be able to astonish and elude the Romans, he put on a white frock and buttoned upon him a purple cloak and appeared out of the ground where the Temple had formerly been." The disguise did not work, and he was sent in chains to Rome to perish after the triumphal march.

Josephus puts the final casualty figures for this siege of Jerusalem at 1,100,000, "for they were come up from all the country to the feast of unleavened bread, and were of a sudden shut up by the army." Of the survivors, "the tallest and most beautiful were reserved for the triumph, those under 17 were sold as slaves and a great many were sent to the provinces to die in the arenas by the sword and wild beasts." Even during the sorting out, 1,100 died for want of food either because the Romans did not give them enough or because they themselves refused to eat. "This was the end which Jerusalem came to by the madness of those that were for innovations; a city otherwise of great magnificence and of mighty fame among all mankind."

The temple of Herod had fallen, and the city that had put to death the Savior of men had virtually destroyed itself. Inconceivable changes were to take place on Mount Moriah as the world took its first momentous steps into the Christian era. For the Jews a new dispensation had begun with the passing of that which had been their central point of worship. They were to be scattered now among the nations, but they would take with them their writings and their religion. They would survive because they had a unique role in human history. And the Jerusalem that now lay about them in ruins would rise again because it too was an integral part of that uniqueness.

Having played his part in the drama that was now over, Titus "went down with his army to that Caesarea which lay by the sea-

Relief of Titus's victory procession with spoils and prisoners from the fallen city of Jerusalem. The Titus Arch is still standing in Rome.

side, and there laid up the rest of his spoils in great quantities, and gave order that the captives should be kept there: for the winter season hindered him then from sailing into Italy." He had come, he had seen, and he had conquered. It was time for him to join his father in a joint victory parade, and for the striking of a coin depicting Judea as a woman, bound and weeping, sitting beneath a palm tree.

All quotations are from Josephus, *Wars of the Jews.*

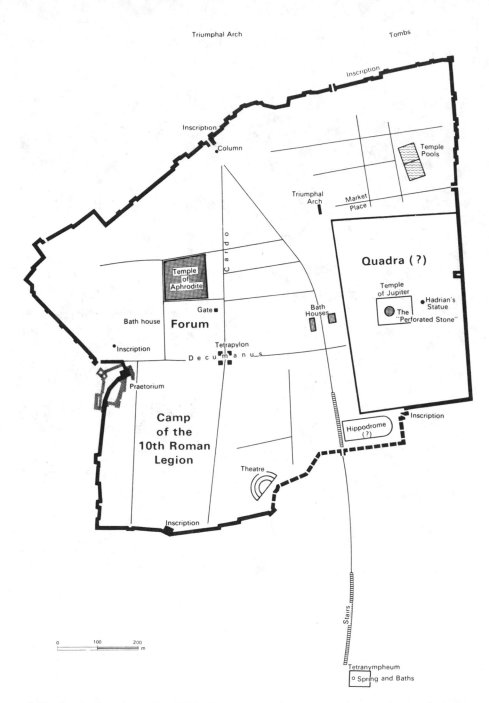

Aelia Capitolina (A.D. 135-300). *Emperor Hadrian wanted Jerusalem to bear his name, thus, "Aelia," part of his complete name Publius "Aelius" Hadriannus, and "Capitolina," referring to the Capitolina triumvirate: Jupiter, Juno, and Minerva.*

24
Persian Fury

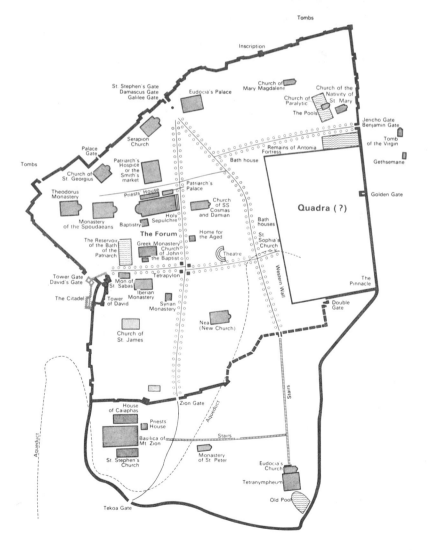

Tombs

Inscription

Church of
Mary Magdalene

St. Stephen's Gate
Damascus Gate   Eudocia's Palace
Galilee Gate

Church of the
Nativity of
St. Mary

Church of
Paralytic

The Pools

Jericho Gate
Benjamin Gate

Palace
Gate

Serapion
Church

Remains of Antonia
Fortress

Bath house

Tomb
of the Virgin

Tombs

Church of
St. Georgius

Patriarch's
Hospice
or the
Smith's
market

Patriarch's
House

Patriarch's
Palace

Gethsemane

Golden Gate

Theodorus
Monastery

Church
of SS
Cosmas
and Damian

Quadra (?)

Monastery
of the Spoudaeans

Holy
Sepulchre

Baptistry

The Forum

Bath
houses

St
Sophia's
Church

The Reservoir
of the Bath
of the
Patriarch

Greek Monastery
Church
of John
the Baptist

Home for
the Aged

Theatre

Tower Gate
David's Gate

Mon of
St. Sabas

Tetrapylon

Iberian
Monastery

Western Wall

The Pinnacle

The Citadel

Tower
of David

Syrian
Monastery

Double
Gate

Church of
St. James

Nea
(New Church)

Stairs

House
of Caiaphas

Zion Gate

Priests
House

Aqueduct

Stairs

Basilica of
Mt. Zion

Stairs

St. Stephen's
Church

Monastery
of St. Peter

Aqueduct

Eudocia's
Church

Tetranympheum

Tekoa Gate

Old Pool

I**T IS HARD TO BELIEVE** that sixty years after what they had suffered in Jerusalem in A.D. 70 the Jews were again in open revolt. The years following the siege had seen a trickle of Jews returning to worship at the temple site and the return, too, of the Christians who had stood apart from the national uprising and had fled from the city during the withdrawal of Cestius Gallus's forces. As a political entity, the Jews no longer counted, but Judaism did not disappear with the reduction of the temple to rubble. It took fresh root at Jamina, thirty miles west of Jerusalem where a rabbinical council that replaced the Sanhedrin came into being under the leadership of Johanan ben Zakkai. It assumed responsibility for the preservation and interpretation of the Law and its application to contemporary problems. Instead of priests, there were now scribes and teachers and these began work on a commentary that became known as the Talmud. At Jamina in A.D. 90, the canon of Old Testament Scripture was finally decided upon, with the Apocrypha omitted. It was still his religion that was to be the supreme link in the new Jewish exile.

And it was also from the new caste of scholars that support came for Simon Bar Kochbah in A.D. 132, when the Jews made a last desperate effort to throw off the Roman yoke in a rebellion that came near to equaling in scope and intensity that of A.D. 66. Hadrian, a restless emperor with a zeal for building, had turned his attention to the ruins of Jerusalem. But he was not a Cyrus and any hopes the Jews might have had of a new temple were rudely shattered when they saw a shrine to Jupiter going up on the sacred site. It was all that was needed to start another conflagration.

The small Roman garrison in Jerusalem was disposed of and the city taken over. Guerrilla warfare was waged for three years before Julius Severus brought the country to its knees again. Over half a million Jews died, captives were sold for the price of a horse, and Jerusalem became Aelia Capitolina, a city that was to be accessible only to Gentiles for the next 200 years. This time the Romans were determined to write "finis" to a nation's history, and to all intents and purposes this had been done. The Jews had lost everything of a material nature. They should, by rights, have disappeared from history. But Hadrian was just as wrong in his calculations as was Diocletian some 150 years later when he had the inscription *Extincto nomine Christianorum* ("the name of the Christians having been extinguished") put over the ashes of a copy of the Bible in the tenth and final purge of the Christian churches since Nero. The Jewish people were to survive — but always at a terrible price — and the teaching of a Nazarene carpenter was to cause Eusebius, father of church history to remark, "It cannot be conceived within how short a period the Christian doctrine, under the glorious conduct of its Author, diffused itself over the face of the earth, by the mouths of his evangelists and apostles."

There is irony again in the fact, however, that while Christianity was extending its frontiers far and wide, even to Britain, the city that gave it birth was plunged back into paganism with the doors shut against every Jew. It was not until persecution gave way to toleration throughout the Roman Empire under Constantine that Jerusalem began assuming openly a Christian character and offering herself as an object for pilgrimage. The Edict of Milan (granting civil and religious rights to all Christians) had followed swiftly on Constantine's experience on the eve of the battle of Milvian Bridge, near Rome, in October 312, when he is reputed to have seen a cross in the sky with the words "In this sign conquer." Victory the following day made him emperor of the West, and in 323 victory over Licinius, ruler in the East, made him master of the Roman world. In 324 Christianity became a state religion, and the following year Constantine convened its first general council when three hundred bishops met at Nicaea in Asia Minor. Already there were signs of schism and the simple teachings of the Galilean were beginning to be obscured. Not far off on the shores of the Bosphorus a new capital was being built at Constantinople and in 330 this became the seat of government.

As the fourth century advanced, the transformation of Jerusalem gathered momentum with the building of churches on "identified" holy sites, and for three hundred years its history is wholly ecclesiastical. A pagan temple, covering what tradition alleges was the tomb of Jesus, was replaced by the first Church of the Holy Sepulcher. Other Christian shrines appeared on the Mount of Olives (site of the Ascension), on the supposed site of the Last Supper, and in the Garden of Gethsemane. The Empress Eudocia, wife of Theodosius II, followed Helena, mother of Constantine, in establishing and endowing churches, hospices, and monasteries. She also completed a new wall around Jerusalem that had been started by her husband in 413 and is credited with the building of the now-walled-up Golden Gate directly opposite the Garden of Gethsemane.

It was also under Eudocia that the Jews were given legal status once more in Jerusalem. Some eighty years before, Julian, known as "the Apostate," had come out in favor of the Jews and authorized the rebuilding of the temple. But the venture came to a sudden and dramatic end when gas in an underground passage was ignited by a torch and an explosion rocked the area. No attempt has ever been made since to rebuild the sanctuary, and even with Eudocia's concession Jerusalem was now no longer a Jewish city. It had passed from that to one stamped first by classical paganism, in the days when it was Aelia Capitolina, and then by orthodox Christianity. What Constantine the Great had begun, Justinian (527-565) completed. While the barbarians were sacking Rome and, in 476, putting an end to the Empire in the West, Jerusalem was basking in the last few moments of Byzantine splendor as a Christian metropolis.

Justinian had his attention drawn to Palestine as a result of a Samaritan revolt over taxation that resulted in the destruction of churches outside Jerusalem. These churches were repaired and new ones were built. Pilgrims and wealth poured into Jerusalem until the city, it is said, began to look as it was in the time of Solomon. But there was no Jewish temple. The structure of Byzantine Jerusalem under Justinian is preserved in a mosaic map discovered on the floor of the church at Madaba in Jordan in 1884. It shows the city surrounded by walls and dominated by the Church of the Holy Sepulcher with its golden dome above the rotunda. But the temple area is wasteland — perhaps as an affront to its former occupiers. It was waiting for a Muslim mosque, which was to stand on the sacred site for 1,300 years. But first would come the Persians, with a fury as great as that of the Assyrians. The Empire in the east was to last until

1453, but Jerusalem was to lie in ruins again within 50 years.

Its new desolater was Chosroes II (590-628). His grandfather, Chosroes I, the greatest monarch of the Sassanidae dynasty of Persia, had waged war on the Romans for twenty years. Chosroes II consolidated these years of challenge by overrunning Syria, Palestine, Egypt, and Asia Minor almost to the gates of Constantinople. On May 20, 614 (Titus had begun his siege in the same month 544 years before), history repeated itself on the walls and citizens of Jerusalem, except that this time the Jews were on the side of the victor. The wealth, beauty, and accumulated splendor of three hundred years vanished in a new onslaught that left forty thousand defenders dead. The followers of Zoroaster caused devastation around the city from which, it is said, Jerusalem has never really recovered. Inside, churches were razed, including that of the Holy Sepulcher and the magnificent Saint Mary of the New, built by Justinian. Christendom, like Judaism, lay in the dust of another devastated Jerusalem. Justinian's city had crumbled, just as that of Herod and of Solomon had done. The pattern of Jerusalem's history was not to change with the Christian era. The city was never to escape from the threat and the reality of destruction.

The Persians held Jerusalem for fifteen years during which they permitted a certain amount of rebuilding of churches, the Anastasis (Greek name for the Church of the Holy Sepulcher) getting a new dome and a slightly more modest basilica. Meanwhile the Byzantine Emperor Heraclius (610-641), "of splendid but fitful genius," had reorganized his army and in 622 began a series of brilliantly successful campaigns against his eastern enemy. He eventually drove Chosroes back to his capital of Ctesiphon and compelled him to return the "sacred cross" that the Persian had removed from the Church of the Holy Sepulcher.

In March of 629 Heraclius entered Jerusalem in triumph with the wooden relic and immediately put the Holy City once more out of bounds to the Jews. But the new Byzantine occupation was to last less than ten years. For in the deserts of Arabia had risen a religious and political force that was to fill the vacuum created by exhausted Persian and Eastern Roman empires. By the end of the century an Arab state was to stretch from Spain to the borders of India and its architects were to change, among other things, the face of Jerusalem.

25
Crescent on the Temple Mount

*Dome of the Rock on the Temple Mount with portion of the Western Wall (top);
the famous mosque from the courtyard (bottom).*

JERUSALEM! Some fresh invader was always to be standing at
her gates; there was always to be the alien hand at her throat.
Paganism placed its gods on her temple site. The Persians had
trampled on the Christian shrines. Now the Muslim was to set up his
place of worship on holy ground, and a third faith was to find a home
in Jerusalem. From the seventh century onward, the Dome of the
Rock has dominated the Jerusalem skyline. It was built by one of the
successors to the prophet whose teaching was to challenge Christianity down the centuries.

Muhammad was born in Mecca about the year 570. By the time
he was six, both his parents were dead and he was entrusted to the
care of an uncle. As a result probably of his having to tend the flocks
of sheep and goats on the hills about the city as a boy, he is credited
with remarking that "no prophet has been raised up who did not
perform the work of a shepherd." But the founder of Islam had to
wait until he was forty years old before his first "revelation" came
from God, and another three years before his doctrine began to take
shape in the Koran. There was no God but God, and Muhammad
was his last and greatest prophet, Jesus being but a forerunner and
not the divine Christ of the gospel. Mercy was to be obtained
through fasting, prayer, almsgiving, and the leading of a pious and
moral life. Idolatry could not be countenanced, and it was this tenet
of the new teaching that aroused the fiercest opposition. For many
years the center of attraction in the Great Mosque of Mecca was the
Kaaba, an oblong building that housed several hundred images as
well as the celebrated Black Stone built into its southeast corner.
Thousands made pilgrimages to worship at it.

187

In July of 622 Muhammad was forced to flee his birth place and settled in more friendly Medina. The flight (Hegira) marked the beginning of the Muhammadan era and eight years later the prophet returned as a visitor to Mecca with ten thousand followers and his tenth wife. Idolatry was stamped out, the creed of the Koran took on a more aggressive character and Muhammad's own attitude towards the Jews, who rejected his messianic claims, hardened into bitterness and at times into ruthless persecution. By the time of his death in 632 the faith of Islam had unified the tribes of Arabia and set the stage for their lightning conquest of the East. The Crescent had become not only the enemy of the Cross, but it was soon to rear itself amidst the holiest precincts of Judaism.

All that Heraclius had won back from the Persians was soon to pass into the hands of the Arabs. Damascus fell in 635 to the forces under Caliph Omar, Muhammad's second successor, and a year later in August Byzantine power suffered a decisive defeat at the battle of Yarmuk River, a left-bank tributary of the Jordan. Palestine lay at the mercy of the invaders, with Jerusalem the final prize. This time it was taken without bloodshed. Fairly early in the year 638, on the Mount of Olives, the city was surrendered by Patriarch Sophronius to Omar on terms of remarkable leniency.

On entering Jerusalem, Omar asked to be taken to the temple site, where the sacred rock, it is said, was buried beneath a mass of refuse. The Caliph initiated its cleansing and prayed to Mecca. It was a historic gesture. After lying desolate for more than five hundred years, the temple mount passed into the possession of the descendants of Ishmael, the race from which Herod the Great had sprung. And thirty years later the Gallic bishop of Arculf was able to report: "On the famous spot where once stood the Temple in all its splendour close to the eastern wall of the city the Saracens worship at a square house of prayer roughly built of vertical boards and of large beams erected above the ruins."[1] From this simple structure, capable, however, of holding three thousand people, was later to emerge the unique Dome of the Rock (Qubbat al-Sakhra), incorrectly called the Mosque of Omar.

Rivalry between the Caliphs, it is said, was the reason Abd-al-Malik started to build the Dome in 687. He hoped to divert pilgrimage from Mecca and Medina to Jerusalem. He could also, of course,

---

[1]Michel Join-Lambert, *Ancient Cities and Temples: Jerusalem* (London Elek Books, 1958).

have intended the new shrine to act as a counter to the Church of the Holy Sepulcher, something it has undoubtedly done to this day. The double octagon of exquisitely patterned marble tiles was finished in 691, Malik having "set apart money for the project equivalent to the whole revenue of Egypt for seven years."[2] Supported by Muslim tradition that it was from the Holy Stone beneath the cupola that Muhammad rose to heaven on his black horse, Jerusalem became the Arabs' third most important city, and they called it al-Quds, the Holy Town.

Freedom of worship was enjoyed under the new regime. Christians were allowed to utilize existing churches but were forbidden to build new ones or toring bells. For the Jew there was certain liberty of movement. He could live in his own quarter, worship in his synagogues, and lament at the Wailing Wall. But, as in the days of Hadrian, there was no joy for him in the temple mount, now to be known as the Haram es-Sharif, the Enclosure of the Noble Sanctuary. What Christendom had spurned, Islam had grasped with willing hands. And for a while Jerusalem experienced a measure of peace and prosperity with the Muslims reducing the city walls to something like their present-day dimensions, and forcing the inhabitants to move from steep slopes northward to more level ground. With the removal of the Arab capital from Damascus to Baghdad, however, and a change from the Unmayed to the Abbasid dynasty in 750, a period of slow decline set in.

Tension between the different religious communities at times erupted into open warfare, and in 969 Jerusalem fell under the power of the Fatimid Caliphs of Egypt, from whose line came the infamous El-Hakim. In sharp contrast to Omar's humane conquest, Hakim's period of devastation began in 1009 with the destruction of the Church of the Holy Sepulcher and some thirty thousand other churches throughout Palestine and Asia Minor. Persecution of Jews and Christians did not cease until seven years later when Hakim declared himself an incarnation of God, and for the next few decades Jerusalem was left to its own devices.

But already the Seljuk Turks had appeared on the distant horizon, pressing south and west from Central Asia. In 1071 they won a battle against the Byzantine army at Manzikert in Armenia that was to point the way to the Ottoman capture of Constantinople nearly

---

[2]Walter Besant and E. H. Palmer, *Jerusalem: City of Herod and Saladin* (London: Chatto & Windus, 1899).

four hundred years later. Jerusalem's fall in 1077 to this cruel, warlike people marked the beginning of yet another long blood-stained chapter in her history. For in the wake of the Seljuks were to come the Crusaders bent on revenge and regaining from the "infidels" the holy sites and shrines of Christendom.

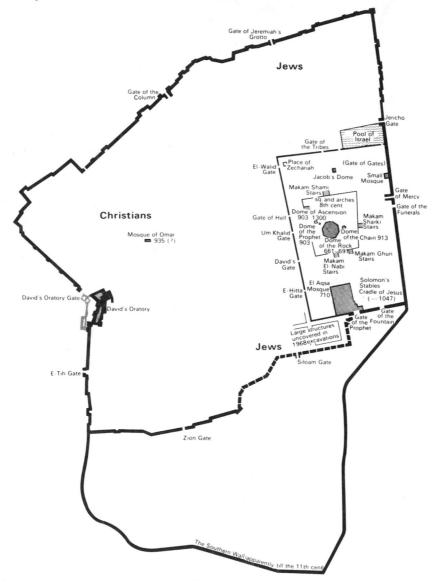

Jerusalem in the first Moslem Period (A.D. 640-1099).

26
Kingdom of the Crusaders

Scratchings by crusader pilgrims in lower level of the Church of the Holy Sepulchre.

IT WAS INEVITABLE, perhaps, that the deteriorating position of the Christians in the Holy Land, first under Caliph Hakim and then under the Seljuk Turks should produce a reaction from the West. Oppression in various forms and denial of access to venerated sites combined to set in motion a train of events that, whatever the ultimate benefits, stained at once and forever the image of Christendom. The backlash that was the answer to the religious crisis in Palestine came in the form of the Crusades.

Nearly three hundred years had passed since Charlemagne had encouraged large-scale pilgrimage to Jerusalem and endowment of church buildings, and it was felt that events had reached a stage when drastic action was necessary to preserve this heritage. Long before, writing from monastic seclusion in Bethlehem in 386, Jerome had recorded that "the Britons who live apart from our world, if they go on pilgrimage, will leave the western parts and seek Jerusalem known to them by fame only, and by the Scriptures."

But the time had now come when Britons were to entangle themselves in a less pious way in the affairs of a little country in the Middle East and to join the rest of Europe in a bid to reestablish the right of entry to Christianity's hallowed shrines. It had been quite useless for Gregory of Nyssa to declare that pilgrimage itself achieved nothing, for Augustine to teach that God was approached far better by love than by travel, and even Jerome himself to observe that heaven could be reached as easily from Britain as from Jerusalem. Soon there was to echo throughout Europe the cry "Deus vult, Deus vult!" ("God wills it") and Christendom was to unite as it has never done since in strength against the "infidel" in the East.

It has been claimed that the Crusades saved the West from the Turks and were the means of widening the horizons of mankind. Not all who promoted them and certainly not all who took part in them were motivated by religious fervor. A chance was seen by Christendom to unite the warring feudal lords in a common cause, with the spoils in distant lands, and spiritual blessings for all who went forth to fight. There was everything to be gained by marching under the banner of the Cross and believing that their campaigning was the will of God. But the walls of the cities that the Crusaders surrounded did not, like those of Jericho long ago, fall down at the sound of a trumpet. The "holy war" was a long and costly one, resulting in an appalling loss of life and in the first major disaster to the Jews in Europe. It began soon after William of Normandy had made himself master of Anglo-Saxon England, and it was an English king, Richard Coeur de Lion, who was one of the leaders of the Third Crusade. Strange and terrible things were to happen again in and around Jerusalem as the world settled down to its second thousand years of the Christian era.

The rumblings began in 1075 with an appeal by Byzantine Emperor Michael to Pope Gregory VII for help against the Turks, but it was not until twenty years later that the marching eastwards actually commenced. At a Council at Clermont in France Pope Urban II called for action, and emissaries were soon holding vast audiences captive with emotional oratory. Their preaching met with almost instantaneous success. By the spring of 1096 four separate and disorderly contingents numbering, all told, about 300,000 people had set off for the Holy Land. Only nine or ten knights were among the host of peasants, brigands, and general riff-raff that gathered on the banks of the Meuse under the leadership of Walter the Penniless. Most of these got no farther than Bulgaria, where they were massacred.

Peter the Hermit, at the head of some 40,000 men, women, and children, succeeded in reaching Constantinople with about half that number. Most of these perished at the hands of the Turks when they got to Nicaea. Gottschalk, a German monk, led 15,000 of his countrymen to their doom in Hungary where another 200,000-strong rabble group also met its end after taking the life of every Jew it came across. These are the sad and imponderable facts of history, and it was only after such senseless and disastrous expeditions that the feudal lords and barons of the West, speaking some twenty different languages, began their two-year march to Jerusalem.

Taking Nicaea in June 1097, it was not until the end of that year that they laid siege to Antioch, in Muslim hands since 635 but still basking in a reflected glory from the time it was the world's third metropolitan city under the Romans. In this pleasantly situated city on the south bank of the Orantes River and only fifteen miles from the Mediterranean, the disciples were first called Christians, and the first gentile church was founded; from here Paul set out on his three great missionary journeys. Justinian rebuilt Antioch after its destruction by earthquake in 526 and the walls he built were to help Islam defy 300,000 adherents of Christendom for six months. Their ranks thinned by famine and disease, the Crusaders eventually penetrated the city on June 3, 1098, slew its defenders, and then, in turn, found themselves besieged by 200,000 Muslims sent by the Persian sultan. Three weeks later these Muslims were routed and the way lay open to the great objective three hundred miles to the south.

Led by Godfrey de Bouillon and his brother Baldwin, fewer than fifty thousand Crusaders caught their first glimpse of Jerusalem on June 6, 1099, almost exactly two years to the day after they had taken Nicaea. Once again the city that no nation could permanently destroy was to come under siege and know the horror of its aftermath. After six weeks and several processions by pilgrims around the walls, assault equipment was concentrated on weak spots in the defense and on the morning of July 16, 1099, entry was effected at these points. What followed has remained forever an ineradicable stain on Crusader history. In the area where Jesus had walked as a boy and taught as the Son of man, where Christianity had its beginnings, which had been sacred to the Jew since the time of David and to the Muslim now for over four hundred years, blood flowed up to the knees of horses as the conquerors pursued the Saracens in the enclosure of the Noble Sanctuary. Jews who had escaped the sword were burned to death in their synagogues. No one knows quite how many perished in Jerusalem that day, but it is generally agreed that mercy was altogether absent.

And now an extraordinary experiment was to be conducted in Palestine. For nearly one hundred years feudalism was to hold sway to the land of the Bible. Kings were to reign from Jerusalem and lords and barons were to divide the country among themselves. Although Godfrey de Bouillon was unanimously elected the first king of Christian Jerusalem he "refused to wear a crown of gold in the city where

Christ had worn a crown of thorns," and took instead the title of
Defender of the Holy Sepulcher. Much that is creditable surrounds
the character of this knight, said to be the noblest of the Crusaders.
He died of fever at the age of fifty-four and was buried in the Church
of the Holy Sepulcher with his sword, "more trenchant than King
Arthur's Excalibur." It was Godfrey who began the famous "As-
sizes," the feudal code that governed and guarded all manner of
people going, coming, and dwelling "in the Kingdom of Jerusalem."
These laws, one set for the nobles and another for the bourgeoisie,
were kept in the Church of the Holy Sepulcher and could only be
opened in the presence of nine people, including the king and the
patriarch (i.e., bishop).

Godfrey was succeeded in 1100 by his brother Baldwin I, who
was crowned on Christmas Day, but it was not until the reign of Fulk
of Anjou (1131-1144) that the frontiers of the Latin kingdom reached
their maximum, stretching from Beirut in the north to the Negev
Desert in the south and from the coastal cities to beyond the Jordan
on the east. A language resembling Norman French was spoken.
Pilgrims flocked in their thousands to the Holy Land, braving the
dangers, first of pirates at sea and later of the unruly sections of the
populace on land. The journey from Jaffa (main port of entry) to
Jerusalem took two days and was, according to an English pilgrim of
the year 1102, "a hazardous business. For the Saracens, always
laying snares for the Christians, lie hidden in the hollow places of the
mountains, and the caves of the rocks . . . on the lookout for those
who have lagged behind their party through weariness . . . and
what a number of bodies lie beside the road, torn by beasts."[1]

But such perils did nothing to deter intrepid travelers. And with
the great influx of pilgrims from as far away as Russia and Scan-
dinavia came a building "boom" in Jerusalem. Nearly forty new or
reconstructed churches were functioning after thirty years of
Crusader rule, and many examples of this architectural activity remain to this day, not the least of which is the Church of the Holy
Sepulcher. It was during this strange period of history that the two
famous orders of the Knights Hospitalers (or Knights of St. John of
Jerusalem) and the Knights Templars were founded in Jerusalem.

Both orders were created to guard and care for the sick and
needy Christian pilgrims, becoming later the most formidable military instruments of the Crusaders. When Godfrey moved from tem-

[1]Zev Vilnay, *Israel Guide* (Jerusalem, 1973), p. 70.

porary quarters in the Al-Aqsa mosque south of the Dome of the Rock to the vicinity of the Citadel at the Jaffa Gate, the Templars took over the temple area. They placed a cross on the Dome, surrounded the sacred rock with iron railings and made this Muslim shrine their religious headquarters for the next eighty years. They kept their horses in underground vaults that formed, in the southeast corner, part of the huge platform thrown out by Herod to enlarge the sanctuary area.

But the cross was not to remain for long above what the Crusaders thought was Solomon's temple. Muslim conquests of Edessa, another Latin kingdom in Syria, led to consternation in Europe and the launching of the Second Crusade. This time two great armies, with a united strength estimated at over one million were under the command of Louis VII of France and the Germanic Emperor Conrad III. Both armies suffered heavily at the hands of the Turks in Asia Minor, made an unsuccessful and politically ill-advised attack on Damascus, and only a remnant of the once mighty force got itself back to Europe. Islam was once again on the attack, and when a young Kurdish chief called Saladin succeeded in uniting Syria and Egypt under one authority, the days of the kingdom of Jerusalem were numbered. Dissensions among the Franks helped his cause, but it was the breaking of a pact that had guaranteed the safety of pilgrims proceeding to Mecca that led to full-scale war.

On July 4, 1187, in the shadow of a twin-peaked mountain called the Horns of Hattin and practically within sight of the Sea of Galilee, the Turks virtually put an end to Crusader power in Palestine. The king of Jerusalem, Guy de Lusignan, was captured, but his life was spared. Driving south, Saladin found the gates of Caesarea, Nablus, Jaffa, and Jericho open to him, and by September 20 was at the walls of Jerusalem. After transferring his siege equipment from the west to near the Gate of St. Stephen on the east where the Kidron Valley has less depth, he began the assault. On October 2 the city surrendered.

This time there was no massacre. Saladin followed the example of Caliph Omar, and Jerusalem was spared another blood bath. The wealthy were able to buy their freedom, and Jew and Christian settled down to make the best of a tolerant, new regime. That there should be no mistake about Islam having regained the city, however, one of the first acts of the new conquerors was the removal of the cross from the Dome of the Rock. Today, after nearly eight hundred years, the crescent still dominates the temple area.

With the loss of Jerusalem, the Christian kingdom in Palestine was reduced to a narrow coastal strip, but within two years three new armies were making their way east. Of the seven Crusades the third is perhaps the best remembered, mainly because of its colorful leaders — Frederick Barbarossa of Germany, Philip of France, and England's Richard "the Lionhearted." In the last-named, Saladin was to meet his match in valor if not in diplomacy. The Crusade failed in its objective of recapturing Jerusalem, but it won the kingdom a respite of another one hundred years. Although Frederick was thrown from his horse and drowned in a river in Silesia, his forces went on to join Richard and Philip at Acre, which became the Crusaders' pivotal city from then on.

King Philip returned to France, and Richard began a victorious march southwards along the coast before turning toward Jerusalem. The supreme prize eluded him, but his prodigious feats of valor gained him the admiration of his foes and a treaty with Saladin by which "the people of the West were to be at liberty to make pilgrimages to Jerusalem, exempt from the taxes which the Saracen princes had formerly imposed."[2] Which was, indeed, nothing less than what the first Crusaders had set out to secure. Richard sailed for Europe in October 1192, was held to ransom for $400,000 by the emperor of Germany for two years, and spent the rest of his days fighting the king of France. He died from an arrow wound while attacking a castle in 1199. Saladin, his chivalrous adversary in the east, died in 1193 at the age of fifty-six and was buried in Damascus in a modest tomb with the prayer inscribed above it that God would open the gates of heaven to his spirit, the last victory for which he hoped.

Though several more Crusades were launched during the thirteenth century, none of them achieved anything except that of the German Emperor Frederick II, excommunicated for taking too long in setting off. But it was this sovereign who, seizing his chance when Egypt and Damascus were at loggerheads, won back Jerusalem in 1229 purely by negotiation. In a ten-year treaty with the Sultan of Egypt he secured not only Jerusalem (except for the temple area) but also Jaffa, Nazareth, and Bethlehem. After having himself crowned in the Church of the Holy Sepulcher, he returned with some justifiable satisfaction to Europe, only to find himself even more out of favor with Pope Gregory IX than before.

---

[2]*Chamber's Encyclopedia* (London: Waverley, 1930), vol. 3.

But this decade of comparative tranquillity in Palestine was the calm before the storm. In 1244 a Tatar tribe called the Khwarizmians, driven south from Lake Aral in Central Asia by Ghengis Khan, swept through Syria and put Jerusalem to the sword. Expeditions under Louis IX of France and Edward I of England (the last of the Crusaders) failed to regain any lost ground, and with the fall of Tripoli in 1289 and Acre in 1291, an era was over. The Knights finally took their departure, leaving the East and their incomparable feudal fortresses to the Muslims.

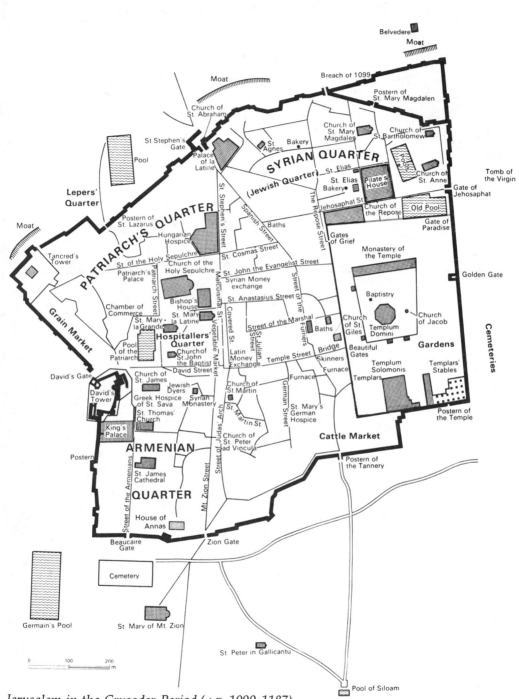

Belvedere

Moat

Breach of 1099

Postern of
St. Mary Magdalen

Church of
St. Abraham

Moat

St. Stephen's
Gate

Pool

Church of
St. Mary
Magdalen

Church of
St. Bartholomew

St.
Agnes

Bakery

SYRIAN QUARTER

Palace
of la
Latine

(Jewish Quarter)

St. Elias

St. Elias
Bakery

Pilate's
House

Church of
St. Anne

Tomb of
the Virgin

Lepers'
Quarter

Postern of
St. Lazarus

PATRIARCH'S QUARTER

Hungarian
Hospice

Jehosaphat St.

Church of
the Repose

Old Pool

Gate of
Jehosaphat

Gate of
Paradise

Moat

Baths

Gates
of Grief

St. Cosmas Street

Monastery of
the Temple

Golden Gate

Tancred's
Tower

St. of the Holy
Sepulchre

Church of the
Holy Sepulchre

St. John the Evangelist Street

Syrian Money
exchange

Baptistry

Patriarch's
Palace

Bishop's
House

St. Anastasius Street

Chamber of
Commerce

St. Mary
la Latine

St. Mary
la Grande

Street of the Marshal

Street of the Furriers

Church
of St.
Giles

Templum
Domini

Church
of Jacob

Cemeteries

Pool
of the
Patriarch

Hospitallers'
Quarter

Church of
St. John
the Baptist

David Street

Latin
Money
Exchange

Baths

Temple Street

Beautiful
Gates

Skinners

Furnace

Templum
Solomonis

Gardens

Templars'
Stables

David's Gate

Church of
St. James

Jewish
Dyers

Church of
St. Martin

German Street

Bridge

Furnace

Templars

David's
Tower

Greek Hospice
of St. Sava

Syrian
Monastery

St.
Martin St.

St. Mary's
German
Hospice

Postern of
the Temple

St. Thomas'
Church

King's
Palace

ARMENIAN

Church of
St. Peter
ad Vincula

Cattle Market

Postern

St. James
Cathedral

QUARTER

Postern of
the Tannery

House of
Annas

Beaucaire
Gate

Zion Gate

Cemetery

Germain's Pool

St. Mary of Mt. Zion

St. Peter in Gallicantu

0   100   200
m

Pool of Siloam

Jerusalem in the Crusader Period (A.D. 1099-1187).

27
Decay and Decline

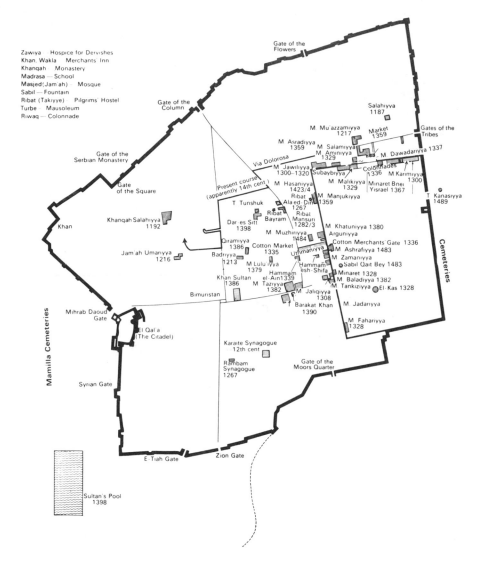

Zawiya — Hospice for Dervishes
Khan, Wakla — Merchants' Inn
Khanqah — Monastery
Madrasa — School
Masjed (Jam'ah) — Mosque
Sabil — Fountain
Ribat (Takiyye) — Pilgrims' Hostel
Turbe — Mausoleum
Riwaq — Colonnade

Gate of the Flowers

Gate of the Column

Gate of the Serbian Monastery

Gate of the Square

Salahiyya 1187

M. Mu'azzamiyya 1217
Market 1359
Gates of the Tribes

M. Asradiyya 1359
M. Salamiyya
M. Aminiyya 1329
M. Dawadariyya 1337

Via Dolorosa

M. Jawiliyya 1300–1320
Subaybiyya
M. Karimiyya 1300
Colonnades 1336
M. Malikiyya 1329
Minaret Bnei Yisrael 1367

Present course (apparently 14th cent.)

M. Hasaniyya 1423/4
Ribat Ala ed-Din 1267
M. Manjukiyya 1359

T. Kanasiyya 1489

T. Tunshuk
Ribat Bayram
Ribat Mansuri 1282/3

Khan

Khanqah Salahiyya 1192

Dar-es Sitt 1398

M. Khatuniyya 1380
Arguniyya

Cotton Merchants' Gate 1336
M. Ashrafiyya 1483

M. Muzhiriyya 1484

Qiramiyya 1386
Cotton Market 1335

M. Zamaniyya
Sabil Qait Bey 1483

Jam'ah Umariyya 1216

Badriyya 1213
Uthmaniyya

Hammam esh-Shifa
Minaret 1328
M. Baladiyya 1382

M. Lulu'iyya 1379
Hammam el-Ain 1339

M. Tankiziyya
El-Kas 1328

Khan Sultan 1386
M. Taziyya 1382

M. Jaliqiyya 1308
M. Jadariyya

Bimuristan

Barakat Khan 1390

M. Fahariyya 1328

Cemeteries

Mamilla Cemeteries

Mihrab Daoud Gate

El Qal'a (The Citadel)

Karaite Synagogue 12th cent.

Gate of the Moors Quarter

Rambam Synagogue 1267

Syrian Gate

E-Tiah Gate
Zion Gate

Sultan's Pool 1398

Not On the Map

IT HAS BEEN SAID that for the next five hundred years Jerusalem passed out of history. Though a little sweeping perhaps, the observation squares pretty well with the facts. For centuries this enigmatical city had been the center of wanton destruction, wars, and conflicting ideologies. The star, the cross, and the crescent were now part of her religious makeup. Her whole history, it has also been suggested, was meant to teach the lesson of humility. No sooner had she risen on the ruins of a former splendor than she was brought low again. But now there was to be a long period of sterility. It came in the wake of the Mongol depredations and proceeded virtually unchecked through 267 years of Mameluke and 400 years of Ottoman rule. By the middle of the seventeenth century Palestine's economic decline had practically touched rock bottom, and by the nineteenth century the land had taken on the appearance of an empty desert.

The Mamelukes (from the Arabic word *mamluk* meaning "owned") were soldier-slaves who eventually became the rulers of Egypt in succession to the Fatimid Caliphs and the weak Ayyubids. The Caliphs of Baghdad initiated the practice of buying Turkish-speaking people from the Caucasus and Central Asia to act as bodyguards and to protect them from rivals. The idea caught on and Egyptian sultans and emirs in Cairo were soon competing in an open market for the best and strongest Mamelukes. In 1250 the dangers in the practice crystallized with the servant taking over from the master. From then until their defeat at the hands of the Ottoman Turks in 1517, forty-eight different Mamelukes from two dynasties ruled Egypt, Syria, and Palestine. Might was right, and treacherous assassinations marked the period. But in many aspects of administration and in the field of engineering, the Mamelukes were in advance of their times. They reveled in pomp and pageantry and were generous patrons of the arts.

Under the Mamelukes, Islamic mosques and madrases (Muslim theological colleges) multiplied in Jerusalem, while Christians had difficulty in maintaining what they had. Exorbitant taxes forced pilgrims to cut short their stay, and the general economy of the city remained precarious. Total population at the end of the fifteenth century is estimated at no more than fifteen thousand, of which one thousand were probably Christians and three hundred Jews — a far cry from the number of inhabitants that watched the legions of Titus encompass the city. Writing about Palestine in 1267, where he arrived a few years after the Mongol invasion, a rabbi had this to say: "How shall I describe our country? It is forsaken and desolate. The holier the place, the greater its state of neglect. Jerusalem is the most desolate locality." The picture is a pathetic one, but it was one that fitted a prophecy.

The Holy City was to know its own sorrow. But the realization that this once proud Jewish capital had become the prey of every dominant nation did not stop there. The Jew in exile knew from the accounts of travelers that the whole of Palestine was slowly becoming a stony, cactus-covered waste, where "there was burning instead of beauty" (Isa. 3:24). And he knew that this is what his prophets had foretold with an accuracy that made him cling more tightly to what persecution had failed to deprive him of — the inspired Chronicle of his history and his laws, faithfully and scrupulously transcribed down the centuries. He was also acutely aware that except for the Latin Kingdom of the Crusaders, no new state had ever been established in Palestine. It had never been more than a vassal province of a power that ruled it from afar, while always he had continued to pray, "Next year in Jerusalem."

Much water was to flow down the Jordan before that was to happen, and the pattern of persecution that marked the early Crusaders' journey through the Rhineland was to be repeated in more ghastly colors in the years to come. But hope was never to be entirely quenched in the Jewish soul and Jerusalem was always to be there, waiting for the return of the dispersed.

The Mamelukes passed and the Ottoman Turks took their place as masters of the Holy Land. Conquests in the Balkans and Asia Minor were temporarily halted by Tamerlane, but by 1444 the Ottomans were firmly in control of eastern Europe. Their capture of Constantinople in 1453 put an end to an ailing Byzantine Empire and strengthened their position enormously. The Crimea, Greece, Syria, and then the Mamelukes of Egypt were swept into the Turkish net and by 1520 Selim I was able to proclaim himself Caliph of the entire Muslim world. But it was his son, known to the West as Suleiman the Magnificent (1520-66), who rescued Jerusalem from obscurity. So unimportant had the city become by this time that its possession by the Turks in 1516 passed almost unnoticed. Its only source of revenue seemed to be the manufacture of soap and a quantity of religious objects. With its fortifications practically in ruins, the city was more or less at the mercy of pillaging Bedouins.

Suleiman set about rectifying this by rebuilding the walls of Jerusalem and improving the city's water supply. Conduits bringing water from Solomon's Pools near Bethlehem were widened and four public fountains were constructed. The work created great interest among the Jews, one of them recording that "Suleiman the King had set out to build the walls of Jerusalem, the Holy City in the land of Judah . . . with gates and towers as in bygone days. And his fame spread throughout the land, for he wrought a great deed. His workmen also extended the tunnel into the town lest the people thirst for water."[1] Inscriptions on different parts of the wall that surrounds the Old City today indicate that it was built between 1537 and 1541.

But this period of brief activity was but the prelude to a long era of social and economic decline in Jerusalem and a decay that overspread Palestine. While in the main there was religious toleration, tax burdens were crippling and it was only through contributions from abroad that Jews, who had by the middle of the sixteenth century increased to about fifteen hundred, were able to exist in their former capital. The Christians now numbered possibly about the same and the Muslim authorities were called at times to keep the peace among the eight or nine different communities, each of which had its own portion of the Church of the Holy Sepulcher. If the plight of those in Jerusalem and other towns was precarious, that of the tillers of the soil was no less so. The peasant (fellaheen) who tried to make a living from the land was taxed out of existence, or robbed of whatever he had by nomads who thrived in conditions of anarchy.

Because of a tax on every sort of tree, there was hardly one left in

---

[1]Chronicle of Joseph ha-Kohen, *Jerusalem: Israel Pocket Library* (Jerusalem: Keter, 1973), p. 77.

Palestine by the end of the nineteenth century. The country surrounding Acre, according to one report was "a vast and spacious
ruin . . . and most villages were contemptible." Jericho, once re-
nowned for its famous palm and balsam plantations was, in 1850,
treeless and deserted. Wells were choked with rubbish and erosion
was rife, while constant warfare between sheiks resulted in senseless destruction of crops, and nomadic tribes who ruled the Negev
plundered the surrounding country. Although there were periods of
respite, none of them were long enough to reverse the downward
trend or check the diminishing population, which by 1850 had fallen
below 200,000.

By that time another would-be conqueror of the Promised Land
had come and gone. In the spring of 1799, Napoleon Bonaparte, after
his defeat at the Battle of the Nile, led his forces north as Vespasian
had done 1,700 years before. The Corsican took Jaffa in March but
was repulsed by a Turko-British force at Acre. A victory in the plain
of Jezreel brought the French to Nazareth, and here the invaders
stopped. Jerusalem eluded Napoleon as it had done the Roman. It
was at the threshold of the Holy City that Napoleon invited the Jews
to join him in the liberation of their country. But the proposal fell, it
seems, on deaf ears, and by June Napoleon had left Palestine forever,
his invasion having merely added to the desolation of the country.

It was the Jews themselves who were to restore the land that "the
locust had eaten." They were to come first in a tiny trickle and then in
an irresistible tide of humanity. They would come because their God
had said that "he would set his hand the second time to recover the
remnant of his people . . . the outcasts of Israel and . . . the dispersed of Judah from the four corners of the earth" (Isa. 11:11,12).
The first regathering out of exile had been from Babylon, but this
time it was to be from all the nations of the earth. Moses had told
them that they would be scattered from "one end of the earth even
unto the other" (Deut. 28:64) and that God said, "I will make your
cities waste, and bring your sanctuaries unto desolation, and I will
not smell the savour of your sweet odours . . . and ye shall have no
power to stand before your enemies" (Lev. 26:31,37). Nehemiah had
rebuilt the walls of Jerusalem and Zerubbabel their second temple.
Then, in due season someone had come who had called Himself their
Messiah and who had said that their temple would be destroyed
again and they would "fall by the edge of the sword and . . . be led
away captive into all nations" (Luke 21:24). The Romans had proved

themselves an efficient instrument in the fulfilling of this prophecy. For centuries there "was a land without a people and a people without a land."

But immense and dramatic changes were on the way as man slowly freed himself from some of the shackles of the Middle Ages. Even in the darkest days there was always a vital microcosm of Jewish life in Palestine, a surety, as it were, that the multitudes would at some future time return to the land of their forefathers.

And only in the wake of a trail of Jewish blood across the globe was this to take place. Not long after the roving Crusaders had rudely shattered their comparative security in Europe, England closed her doors to the Jews in 1290. They found a haven in France, but by the end of the fourteenth century that country was no longer safe for them. When a bubonic plague, the Black Death, spread from the east, the Jews were accused of poisoning the wells and the rivers, and whole communities were put to death in Germany. Spain became a place of refuge until the Inquisition turned it into a place of torment. An edict under Ferdinand of Aragon and Isabella of Castille gave them three months to leave the country and thus scattered the most prosperous Jewish community in Europe.

By 1492 the roads were clogged with a people again seeking somewhere to live and this time the dispossessed were the flower of Jewish aristocracy — its scholars and its men of substance. Some turned east — to Poland, Russia, and Turkey; some reestablished themselves in London; and some found their way to the New World across the Atlantic. And some drifted down to the ancient byways of Jerusalem, Hebron, Tiberius, and Safed, bringing with them their *kabbalistic* interpretation of the Scriptures. But the main stream flowed to eastern Europe where, in 1875, nearly 75 percent of world Jewry (over seven million) was concentrated. Assimilation was then at its height, but a disaster that was to deal this process a reeling blow was around the corner.

In 1881 Czar Alexander II of Russia was assassinated and Jews soon found themselves the target of organized massacres, or what came to be called "pogroms" (from the Russian *gromit* meaning "to destroy unmercifully"). The dream of emancipation faded in the cold dawn of widespread political anti-Semitism. This time the Jew turned west and south, and, like the Iberian Peninsula expulsion, the exodus from Russia was to have far-reaching effects. Between 1880 and 1913 no fewer than 2,000,000 Jews joined the 250,000 then in

America. But even more significant was the migration — though on a smaller scale — to a neglected Turkish province called Palestine where Jewish agricultural enterprises were to begin in earnest.

With the help of modern Zionism — a movement politically, rather than religiously, orientated — the long-cherished hope of a return to the Promised Land was at last to become a reality. But it was to take more than the exhortations of patriots and visionaries to build a new Jerusalem and repopulate the land. For those who still believed that there was a place for them among the Gentiles, Nazi Germany was to provide the answer. And at times perhaps, in that night of terror, some of them might have remembered the words of their prophet Jeremiah: "I will bring them again into their land that I gave unto their fathers. Behold, I will send for many fishers, saith the Lord, and they shall fish them; and after will I send for many hunters, and they shall hunt them from every mountain, and from every hill, and out of the holes in the rocks" (Jer. 16:15,16).

The "fishers" had been sent — the Zionists, with the bait of a new life in Israel. But it had not proved all that palatable. So the hunters came to Germany, and to Austria and Czechoslovakia, and to Poland and Holland, and to Italy and France, and six million Jews perished. But the trickle of exiles returning to their homeland turned into a torrent, swelled by the "Askenazim"from eastern Europe, the "Sephardim" from the countries of the Mediterranean, Jews of Yemen, Iraq, of China, Malaya, and Afghanistan. Palestine was to stir from its long slumber and Jerusalem to spread like a vine across vale and hill.

28
A Modern Prophet

A PART FROM ITS RELIGIOUS significance, one is inclined always to think of old Jerusalem as a city being sheltered behind its ramparts in readiness for the next siege. History does little to dispel this image, but there have been times when the fighting ceased and life returned to normal. Such was the case, it could be claimed perhaps, under the centuries of Turkish rule. If not exactly a period of prosperity, it was at least one of relative peace, which the twentieth century was to shatter with its own brand of vehemence.

To have lived in Jerusalem during the latter half of the nineteenth century would have been to see a city take its first steps out of a long twilight. These were the years when the European powers invaded the precincts of the Ottoman and a forgotten community began to attract attention. Consulates were established, 1841 saw the publishing and printing of the first book in the city, bells began to ring from church towers, and the rights and privileges of the different congregations were confirmed. It was then that old Jerusalem, which had been divided into nearly four equal parts — the Jewish, the Armenian, the Muslim, and the Christian — began to emerge from behind its walls and spill over into the surrounding countryside.

Behind this historic move was the Jewish banker and philanthropist, Sir Moses Montefiore, who was born in 1784, was Sheriff of London when Victoria began to reign in 1837, and who died in 1885. He visited the Holy Land seven times, making his last trip at the age of ninety. The famous windmill that was erected on the plot of ground this benefactor secured for his people on the western slopes of the city — now known as the suburb of Yemin-Moshe — was used

211

as an observation post by the Jews during the War of Independence, and it turns in the breezes from the Judean hills today. The founder of modern Jerusalem also gave liberally towards improving the supply of water, which was then still being taken during drought periods from the Gihon spring in bags of animal skin and sold at outrageous prices. Not long after people began living outside the city walls, the gates, which had always been closed at night, were left open permanently.

In 1865, the Palestine Exploration Fund was launched to explore Jerusalem underground and the city was linked to the coastal plain by telegraph. The following year work began on the construction of a carriage-way to Jaffa, which the Austrian Emperor, Franz Josef, was able to use after he had attended the opening of the Suez Canal in 1869. About ten years later, the French completed the rail link to the coast and a daily train transported passengers to Jaffa in under three hours, if it were running on time. It was then that chapels began to make their appearance on the Mount of Olives and the Russians built the church with five towers shaped like onions near the Garden of Gethsemane. It was also then that General Charles Gordon claimed that what is now known as the Garden Tomb beyond the Damascus Gate was the site of Calvary.

It was during that eventful half-century that for the first time in 1,800 years Jews became a majority in Jerusalem. According to a British Consulate record of 1865, of the eighteen thousand people then living in the city, over nine thousand were Jewish. And this majority was to increase as the ideal of a homeland and total sovereignty within its borders became more feasible with every year that passed. Moses Hess in 1862, and then Leo Pinsker twenty years later after the first wave of pogroms in Poland and Russia, advocated territorial independence as the only solution to the Jewish dilemma. But it was someone born in 1860 in Budapest who took practical steps to turn the dream into reality.

The new prophet who began to make himself heard among dispersed Israel was Theodor Herzl, who had gone to Vienna to study law but found journalism more to his liking. And it was while he was acting as correspondent for his paper in Paris that the trial of Captain Alfred Dreyfus took place. It was not so much the fact that an innocent man had been convicted of treason that affected Herzl as the cry from the crowd afterwards: 'Kill the Jew!'' The words suddenly brought home to him the precarious state in which his people were still living, even in countries that had granted them full emancipation. There seemed only one answer, which this practical dreamer proceeded to provide in his famous 100-page pamphlet, "Der Judenstaat" (The Jewish State) — the acquiring of a national home where the Jews could work out their own destiny. Not all agreed with him, especially many of his fellow Jews in the West, and even publication of his views, regarded by some as "desperate lunacy," was opposed.

But 197 delegates from nearly every country in which Jews had settled met in Switzerland for the first Zionist Congress on August 29, 1897. At the end of that historic meeting, thirty-seven-year-old Herzl wrote in his diary: "At Basle I founded the Jewish State . . . in five years, or at any rate in fifty, the fact will be generally admitted." He did not live to see how accurately time fulfilled his words and the vision he had of a gleaming new city rising in the encircling hills about Jerusalem, and which he described in a book called *Old-New Land.* But he did see some of the fruit of his zeal and labor, for by the turn of the century, Zionist federations were established throughout the world, and Jews in Jerusalem had increased from nine thousand to some thirty thousand out of a total population of fifty thousand.

His great goal, however, of securing Zion for his people, eluded him. Herzl turned first to the German Kaiser, William II, who he thought might have persuaded the Turkish government to agree to the establishment of a Jewish Commonwealth in Palestine. When these negotiations failed, he appealed directly to the Sultan, but without success. Before he died, Herzl approached Britain on this matter. The island of Cyprus, an area in the Sinai Peninsula, and later Uganda in Central Africa, came up for consideration as temporary "asylums" until Palestine became available. Bitter opposition to all these alternatives revealed how inseparable from Jewish hopes and aspirations was the land of Israel itself. This was the country they believed to be theirs by divine promise, and to which they had never renounced their rights. No other land on earth could take its place.

On July 3, 1904, the man who had, in eight brief years, given a movement as old as the Bible itself new life and vigor, died of the last of a series of heart attacks. Forty-five years later his body was taken from Vienna for reburial on a hilltop — Mount Herzl — in the new city he had once seen in his imagination. In the terraces on the hills

below him are the graves of those who fell in 1948, and beyond them
again stretches the dark green memorial to the Six Million.

Within the next decade, and following a new spate of pogroms
in Russia, the Jewish population of Palestine more than doubled. By
1914 it had grown to over ninety thousand, and forty-three agricultural settlements had been established. It was this wave of immigration, the second aliya (the first had taken place just after 1880 and the
third would occur between the First and Second World Wars) that
began to turn a desert into a land of flourishing orange groves and
productive farms. The world had seen the first signs of a modern
miracle and the emergence of Jewry as a "creative force."

Nor was Jerusalem the only town to spread beyond its ancient
limits. In 1909 a frustrated group of pioneers, stirred to action by
Meir Dizengoff, bought thirty-two acres of sand dunes a little distance from the old Arab port of Jaffa. The idea was to establish a new,
wholly Jewish suburb, and digging began at what is now the inter-
section of Rothschild Boulevard and Herzl Street. Twelve years later
the burgeoning village elected its own mayor and separated itself
from the old town. Soon Jaffa became a suburb of Tel Aviv, "the Hill
of Spring," and time was to make her the largest completely Jewish
city in the world, with a population of over 500,000.

But the transformation of a land that the prophet of independence, Theodore Herzl, saw in his mind's eye in the nineteenth
century, was foretold long before him. In 700 B.C. Isaiah had declared
that at the time of the regathering of Israel, "the desert would rejoice
and blossom as the rose" (Isa. 35:1), while two hundred years later
Zechariah wrote that Jerusalem would be "inhabited as towns without walls, for the multitude of men and cattle therein" (Zech. 2:4).

Montefiore, Herzl, and a host of others had been instruments in
the fulfilling of that prophecy. And there would be others even
though the storm clouds gathered over Europe, war halted development in Jerusalem for four years, and Palestine once more echoed to
the tramp of marching feet. From the resulting chaos and carnage on
the battlefields of Ypres, Verdun, the Somme, and the Marne, there
emerged a fragment of paper that became known as the Balfour
Declaration. It was to change the face of a country and the fortunes of
a people.

29
The Gates Swing Open

Foreign Office,
November 2nd, 1917

Dear Lord Rothschild,

I have much pleasure in conveying to you, on behalf of His Majesty's Government, the following declaration of sympathy with Jewish Zionist aspirations which has been submitted to, and approved by, the Cabinet.

'His Majesty's Government view with favour the establishment in Palestine of a national home for the Jewish people, and will use their best endeavours to facilitate the achievement of this object, it being clearly understood that nothing shall be done which may prejudice the civil and religious rights of existing non-Jewish communities in Palestine, or the rights and political status enjoyed by Jews in any other country"

I should be grateful if you would bring this declaration to the knowledge of the Zionist Federation.

Y. in,

Arthur James Balfour

Facsimile of the Balfour Declaration of 2nd November 1917

FOURTEEN DAYS before Christmas, 1917, a British officer walked slowly through the Jaffa gate into Jerusalem and formally accepted the surrender of the city. Its capture had been as bloodless as when Caliph Omar took it in 638, and General Allenby's entry on foot into the Holy City was a gesture of humility. Two days before, December 9, the Turkish mayor, the chief of police, and one or two others had sallied forth, bearing a white flag, and had encountered a couple of British soldiers searching for water. In circumstances as inauspicious as could ever be imagined another new era had dawned for Jerusalem.

It did so at the close of one of the most fateful years in history, with disaster a feature of most of the Allied operations on land. March saw America enter the war as a result of unrestricted German submarine attacks on merchant shipping, and the disposal of Czar Nicholas II following an uprising in Moscow. The Kerensky government kept a reluctant Russia under arms until the Bolshevik Revolution in November when Lenin, now in power, sued for peace with Germany. The Austrians inflicted a humiliating defeat on the Italians at the battle of Caporetto, and to enable the demoralized French armies to regroup, the British launched an offensive near Passchendaele. Before it was over, they had suffered 300,000 casualties, hundreds even drowning in terrain that had been turned into a vast quagmire by autumn rains.

But in the land of the Bible the Egyptian Expeditionary Force was winning. Advancing into Palestine in October, Edmund Allenby took Beersheba on the last day of that month, Gaza on November 7, and Jaffa on the sixteenth. He was in Jerusalem less

217

than a month later and from the steps of the Citadel, on December 11, made it known that in regard to the religious aspect of the city it was simply a matter of "status quo." In a proclamation written in English, French, Italian, Arabic, and Hebrew, he informed the inhabitants that "every sacred building, monument, holy spot, shrine, traditional site, endowment, pious bequest, or customary place of prayer, of whatsoever form of the three religions, will be maintained and protected according to the existing customs and beliefs of those to whose faiths they are sacred."[1]

The new conqueror of Jerusalem had little idea of what lay in store for the quiet city he had just taken without firing a shot and that its days of existing as a remote backwater were over.

From Jerusalem, Allenby moved on to north Palestine through the Pass of Megiddo (he later took the title Lord Allenby of Megiddo) and by October of the following year he had insured the collapse of Turkey through his victories in Syria. In November, exactly eleven months after his capture of Jerusalem, hostilities ended in Europe.

While this fifty-six year-old British soldier was advancing across the Negev, a 117-word document that was to lead to the changing of the face of that very desert was made public in London. The piece of paper, known in history as the Balfour Declaration, was dated November 2, 1917 and contained these momentous words: "His Majesty's Government view with favour the establishment in Palestine of a national home for the Jewish people and will use their best endeavours to facilitate the achievement of this object, it being understood that nothing shall be done which may prejudice the civil and religious rights of existing non-Jewish communities in Palestine. . . ."

Suddenly, in the midst of a world war, a dream had become reality. A major power had switched on a green light that had been out for centuries, and from a window somewhere in England a man looked out on an avenue of horse chestnut trees and smiled. He realized that another incredibly strange chain of events had taken place in the history of his people and that peculiarly material to them was a tree, indigenous to the mountains of Greece and introduced to England about the year 1630. Its seeds were used by the Greeks and the Turks to cure chest disease among horses, but it was Chaim

[1]Harry Charles Luke and Edward Keith-Roach, *The Handbook of Palestine and Trans-Jordan* (London: Macmillan, 1930), p. 28.

Weizmann, a lecturer in chemistry at the University of Manchester, who found a new use for them.

It was to the Jew of Pinsk, as Weizmann liked to call himself, that Britain's Foreign Secretary, Lord Balfour, had revealed the fact that acetone, a vital solvent in the manufacture of explosives, had become unprocurable in England. The position was critical. But soon horse chestnuts were pouring into factories where a process devised by Dr. Weizmann turned them into the desperately needed solvent, and cordite became once more part of the war arsenal. Thirty-one years later, when the new State of Israel was proclaimed, the scientist on whom Herzl's mantle had fallen, and who had seen in the large and handsome horse chestnut tree the answer to a crisis, was elected its first president.

So, while the tide of war rolled across Europe, there came into existence a pledge as fateful and as historic as any associated with the land that Moses saw from Mount Nebo but did not enter. Although seemingly open to different interpretations, the message of the Balfour Declaration was sufficiently explicit to cause jubilation throughout Jewry and to set it firmly and irrevocably on the road back to national independence. In its essence the declaration was seen as a renewal of the promise that had been fundamental to Jewish history since the time of Abraham and not even the fact that its implementation was bound to mark the beginning of a new era of bloodshed for Jerusalem could detract from its appeal.

Under the Treaty of Sevres, Turkey renounced her sovereignty over Palestine and at San Remo in April 1920 the Allied Powers delegated the mandate to Britain, the decision being confirmed two years later by the League of Nations. By then the Hebrew University had already begun to take shape on Mount Scopus and Hebrew had been recognized as an official language. This not only put the seal on Eliezer ben Yehuda's lifelong ambition to bring the language of the Bible and of prayer into common use; it also fulfilled a 2,500-year prophecy of Jeremiah: "As yet they shall use this speech [Hebrew] in the land of Judah and in the cities thereof, when I shall bring again their captivity" (31:23).

It was about this time, too, that Sir Ronald Storrs, the first military governor, who believed that "there could be no promotion after Jerusalem," decreed that all buildings in the city, private and public, should be built or faced with the beautiful local pink limestone. By 1922 Jerusalem had begun its transformation from a neglected Turkish town to a twentieth-century metropolis that was to become the focus of world attention.

For the next fifty years events concerning Jerusalem and the country of which it was again to be the capital moved with a rapidity and in a way that can have few, if any, parallels in history. With the way now open to Jewish immigration, the simmering resentment of the Arab world was not long in turning into open rebellion. Violence erupted at Easter in 1920 and spectacular development west and north of the Old City walls was accompanied by a series of riots. In October of 1933, about the time that the shadow of Adolf Hitler grew larger over Germany and the Nazi Party was swept into power, a general strike was called by the Arabs in Jerusalem. The target of Muslim anger was now, not only the Jews, but the government. In four years 175,000 new settlers had arrived in Palestine, mainly as the result of the rising tide of German persecution, and Jerusalem's population increased to 135,000, of whom 76,000 were Jews. Another general strike was declared by the newly established Arab Higher Committee in 1936, and Britain's answer was a Royal Commission under Lord Peel.

Partition first came to Palestine in 1922 when Transjordan was excluded from the mandated territory and Emir Abdullah, an Arab prince, was installed at Amman. The Peel report recommended the division of western Palestine's 10,000 square miles between the Jews and the Arabs, the former being allocated an area that included Tel Aviv and Haifa on the coast with Jerusalem and Bethlehem falling under a new mandate. While acceptable to neither party, the proposal was significant in that it was the first British document that discussed openly the creation of a Jewish state. During the next two years relationships deteriorated still further, with Jewish traffic to Jerusalem from the coast under constant attack, the Old City itself becoming an operational headquarters for bandits.

By now, however, the world was on the brink of World War II, and in May 1939 Britain issued the White Paper that virtually cancelled the Balfour Declaration. Jewish immigration to Palestine was limited to 75,000 over the next five years, after which it was to be subject to the consent of the Arab majority; land sales to Jews were permitted in only about 1/20 of the country. It also declared that the establishment of a Jewish state in Palestine was contrary to British obligations to the Arabs.

The bombshell could not have come at a worse time, for at that moment millions of Jews in Europe were beginning to realize that they were facing certain destruction. *Many of them might have escaped the gas chambers had the doors been wider open in Palestine.* But when war was declared on September 3, David Ben Gurion, as head of the Jewish Agency in Jerusalem, and later to become the first premier of the State of Israel, offered the services of the entire adult population to the British Army. "Jewish Palestine," he said, "would fight the war as though there was no White Paper, and fight the White Paper as if there was no war." Nor did Jewry elsewhere shirk its responsibilities in the conflict that engulfed most of the world for the next six years. Palestine became an important arsenal and Jerusalem a military headquarters.

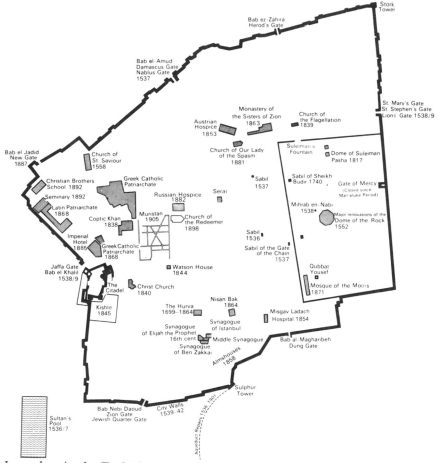

Jerusalem in the Turkish Period (A.D. *1517-1917*).

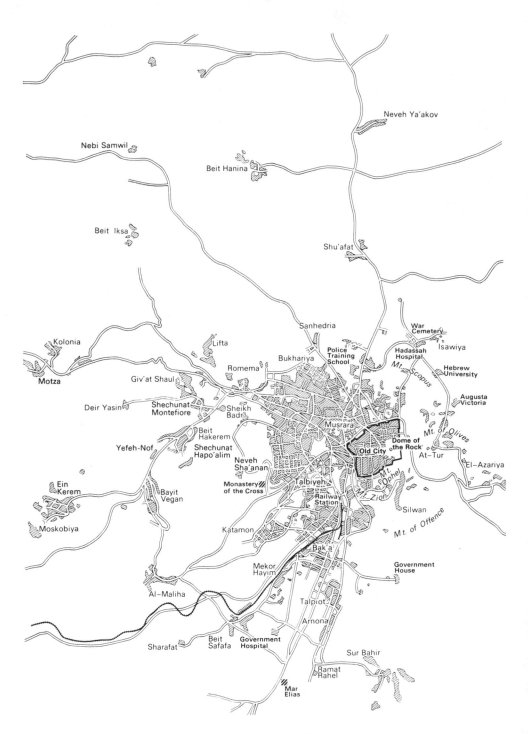

Jerusalem during the British Mandate (1921-1948).

30
Baptism By Fire

Israel fighting through Beersheba in October 1948 (top); repelling enemy action in the hills of Jerusalem during the same month (bottom).

BUT WHEN PEACE CAME to Europe in the middle of 1945, it did not come to the Middle East. The Jews found the gates of their "national home" still only slightly ajar.

During the war and early into 1946 some 40,000 illegal immigrants arrived in Palestine, and on August 12, instructions were given for this to stop. From May 8, 1945, to May 15, 1948, no fewer than seventy-eight ships, many of them rotten, unseaworthy hulks, tried to land refugees on the soil of the Promised Land, and twenty-one succeeded. Haifa, dominated by the eleven-mile-long Carmel range where Elijah had challenged the priests of Baal, became a base for the Royal Navy and 33,000 would-be immigrants were captured and interned on the island of Cyprus. Dissident Jewish forces that had opposed the White Paper of 1939 with violence now went into action to break the blockade of Palestine's coast. They destroyed the radar station at Haifa used to identify the refugees' boats and blew up bridges to hinder pursuit once Jews had landed. The crisis was hastening to a climax.

Violence was once again reddening the streets of Jerusalem. To try to maintain order, Britain imposed curfews and imprisoned and hanged terrorists. In 1947 she decided to relinquish the mandate and took the matter to the United Nations. On November 29, the General Assembly endorsed a partition plan that gave the Jews the coastal plain from Acre to the south of Tel Aviv, eastern Galilee, and practically all the land south and west of Beersheba down to the Gulf of Aqaba. Jerusalem was to come under a Trustee Administration of the United Nations. British rule was to terminate not later than August 1, 1948.

The plan was accepted by the Jews, for it at least recognized their longing for statehood, but the Arab League announced that it would fight partition to the bitter end. For the next six months anarchy prevailed. The Old City was cut off from the new where the British ensconced themselves behind barbed wire in areas from which they had cleared Jewish inhabitants. Mount Scopus, with its Hebrew University and the Hadassah Hospital, became a Jewish-held enclave and was the scene of one of the most tragic incidents of this period of strife. A convoy taking staff to the hospital was attacked and seventy-eight medical personnel were killed. Arab strongpoints straddled the only supply route from the coast and a vital water pipeline was cut.

Jerusalem was again under siege.

At midnight on Friday, May 14, 1948, British civil and military authority came to an end in Jerusalem. But eight hours before — so that the sanctity of the Sabbath should not be affected — about two hundred people had gathered in the Municipal Art Museum on Boulevard Rothschild in Tel Aviv. As the hands of the clock on the wall approached four o'clock, a number of men took their places at a long table immediately beneath the portrait of Theodor Herzl. One of them, who had been born David Green but changed his name to Ben Gurion, began speaking in a silence that might have been prepared by the centuries:

> In the land of Israel the Jewish people came into being. In this land was shaped their religious and national character. Here they lived in sovereign independence. Here they created a culture of national and universal import, and here they wrote and gave the Bible to the world. Though exiled, the Jewish people remained faithful to the land, never ceasing to pray for their return . . . . This has now come about.
> They reclaimed the wilderness, revived their language . . . they sought peace, yet were prepared to defend themselves. They brought the blessings of progress to all inhabitants of the country . . . . By virtue of the natural and historic right of the Jewish people and of the resolution of the General Assembly of the United Nations, *we hereby proclaim the establishment of the Jewish state in Palestine, to be called the State of Israel.*

Soon after the last of the momentous words had died away, the members of the Provisional State Council rose to their feet and sang the Jewish national anthem. The declaration of independence abrogated the terms of the British White Paper, opened the doors of Israel to all Jews, gave approval to the partition plan, and appealed to the Arabs, who were to enjoy equal rights, for peace.

But the baptism of the reborn nation was to follow the pattern of her long history. It was to be by fire.

The war that had started officially seven months before began in earnest at dawn on May 15. While Egyptian planes bombed Tel Aviv, land forces representing some 40,000,000 Arabs launched an invasion of Israel (in which there were now some 650,000 settlers) from every direction except the sea. The Jews met the attack with 35,000 trained troops of the Haganah, three aircraft, homemade mortars, and a "secret weapon" known in Hebrew as *ein brera,* and which in English means "there is no alternative." They also sought inspiration from the past. Their officers discovered in the Bible a valuable military manual. And, as when Joshua first took possession of the land three thousand years ago, miracles were to help them retain it now.

But no miracle was to save the Jewish quarter of old Jerusalem, the sector where Jews had lived for nearly two thousand years beside a fragment of the temple wall. Subjected at first to artillery bombardment from the Mount of Olives, it was captured finally by the Arab Legion on May 27. Before this, a Jewish attack on the Jaffa gate was repulsed, but an armored column of the Legion had been turned back at the Mandelbaum Gate and another column had failed to take the massive hospice of Notre Dame after forcing its way down the Nablus Road. On the other side of the city a handful of Palmach (the elite of the Jewish army), after breaching the Zion Gate and securing a passage into the besieged Jewish sector, had been forced to withdraw.

It was then that the Arab Legion began to move through the heart of old Jerusalem, an explosion ripped apart the beautiful Hurva synagogue, and soon black smoke was billowing above the city. It was the eve of another Jewish Sabbath. Of the 1,700 inhabitants of the Jewish quarter, 1,300 — the women and the aged — were given a safe passage over the five hundred yards to the new city which some entered for the first time. The remaining four hundred Jews became prisoners of war.

The Arab Legion's field guns were now concentrated on the new part of Jerusalem, while one hundred thousand trapped Jews tightened their belts as their rations were cut almost to the vanishing

point. Conditions resembling those when the legions of Titus surrounded the city might have developed but for the discovery of an
ancient track that began somewhere near the Trappist monastery of
Latrun and disappeared into the Judean hills. It was a shepherd's
path to Jerusalem. It by-passed the Arab strongpoint and became the
vital, alternate route to the besieged city. Known as Israel's "Burma
Road," over which convoys from Tel Aviv would somehow manage
to haul their loads of flour, its construction was something of a
miracle. It was also the route that trucks, laden with arms and
ammunition, used to reequip the Israeli forces during the first
cease-fire that began on June 11.

Without it, and without that first invaluable thirty-day truce,
the fate of Jerusalem and the course of events in the Middle East
might perhaps have been very different.

For sixty-six-year-old King Abdullah of Transjordan the lull in
the fighting was also not unwelcome. He would have been happy to
have seen an end to hostilities, and hours after the firing had ceased
around the walls of Jerusalem, he was attending prayers at the El
Aqsa mosque in the temple area. Three years later, on July 20, 1951,
an assassin's bullet ended his life at the same spot. With Abdullah
that day was his sixteen-year-old grandson, Hussein. In deference to
an unusual request of the king, young Hussein had worn a uniform
and various medals. A second bullet struck one of these and glanced
off. Hussein was unharmed and within a year had become king of
the new Hashemite Kingdom of Jordan.

31
Monument To Courage

Kibbutz Yad Mordekhai, founded in 1943 but reduced to ruins in May 1948. It was later rebuilt. The name commemorates Mordecai Anielewicz, commander of the Warsaw Ghetto. His statue is against the background of the water tower, which was destroyed in the fighting of 1948.

WHEN HOSTILITIES were resumed on July 9, Jerusalem was crammed with 7,500 tons of food, 2,800 tons of fuel, and sufficient mortar shells to reduce the Old City to rubble. The tables were turned. In ten days of fighting before the second truce came into effect, the whole war scene began to change, with the Israeli forces taking the offensive and gaining new territory.

But the four-hundred-year-old ramparts of Suleiman the Magnificent were to deny them the most coveted prize of all. A three-pronged attack was launched against them only hours before the cease-fire was due to come into effect. It had been preceded by an artillery barrage that paled the Arab Legion's bombardment of the New City into insignificance. Plans for the administration of the Old City had even been drawn up, so confident were the Jews of success. But it was not to be. The initial assault failed at the Mount Zion sector of the ancient battlements, and there was no time for any other. The 5 A.M. deadline on that seventeenth day of July had beaten the Jews. It was to be another nineteen years before the City of David became theirs.

But success had come elsewhere. Territorial gains made during July were added to when fighting erupted again as the momentous year slid into autumn. With the Egyptian retreat from Beersheba, the Negev lay open to the Israeli forces; in Galilee the Syrians were driven back across their borders. On December 10, the United Nations recognized the existence of the State of Israel, and when, early in 1949, armistices were signed with her enemies, the fledgling was in possession of 23 percent more territory than had been allocated to her by the 1947 partition plan.

231

There was something even a little more than extraordinary about the events of the past nine months. Although the sun did not stand still during the War of Liberation, it is said that the bees fought for Israel when the enemy was approaching Tel Aviv. Swarms of these creatures from the groves east of Petah Tikva, the oldest Jewish agricultural settlement, whose name means "door of hope," attacked the Arabs; Egyptians surrendered when they believed they were surrounded by a vast army; and sickness immobilized a combined Syrian and Lebanese force in Galilee.

When seven nations ranged themselves against Israel in 1948, it was recalled that Joshua began his conquest of the Promised Land with exactly that number to contend with: the Hittites, the Girgashites, the Amorites, the Canaanites, the Perizzites, the Hivites, and the Jebusites — all "greater and mightier than thou," he was informed. The forces of the five kings of the Amorites were dealt with the day the sun stood still above Gibeon, and the "moon in the valley of Ajalon . . . for the Lord fought for Israel" (Josh. 10:12-14). And when the Jewish lines bent under the first, swift onslaughts in 1948, the promise of victory to a former generation must, somewhere in the darkness, have been remembered: "If thou shalt say in thine heart, These nations are more than I; how can I dispossess them? thou shalt not be afraid of them. . . . Moreover *the Lord thy God will send the hornet among them,* until they that are left, and hide themselves from thee, be destroyed" (Deut. 7:17,18,20).

To believe that the Jew, in his twentieth-century fight for survival and independence, was not without allies would not seem very difficult. Nor would it detract from the miracles he has wrought with his own hands and the magnitude of his own sacrifices. The price of sovereignty was high. All told, about six thousand Jews died in securing it, and it has been pointed out that on a proportional basis this would have equaled two million Americans — more than were killed in two world wars.

And if the war against Rome had its Masada, that of 1948 against the Arab world had its Yad Mordekhai. Not that this kibbutz was unique in its heroism. It was only one of many, almost absurdly vulnerable in its isolation, but whose answer when the test came was never in doubt, as that of Jerusalem was clear later when siege guns blew her citizens to pieces.

Today Yad Mordekhai with its giant statue of the hero of the Warsaw ghetto revolt in 1943 (Mordecai Anielewicz, *yad* being the

Hebrew word for "monument") in front of an overturned water tower, lies squarely on the coastal tourist route to the Negev, for the Israelis have reconstructed a battlefield there.

This was once the territory of the Philistines — with its cities of Ashdod, Ashkelon, Ekron, Gath, and Gaza — where the desert really begins. To Ashdod they brought the captured ark of the covenant and next day found that the great image of their god Dagon had fallen on its face. Here the modern descendants of their conquerors are constructing a deep-water harbor that will surpass Haifa. "The beauty of Israel is slain upon thy high places; how are the mighty fallen!" lamented David long ago over the killing of King Saul and the beloved Jonathan by the ancient enemy of the Israelites. "Tell it not in Gath, publish it not in the streets of Ashkelon, lest the daughters of the Philistines rejoice" (2 Sam. 1:19,20). It was in Gaza that the blinded Samson, bound with fetters of brass but given strength for one more feat, pulled down the pillars of the temple of Dagon, and three thousand Philistines perished with him.

In the summer of 1948 the little Jewish settlement of Yad Mordekhai, half-way between Ashkelon and Gaza, blocked the path of an Egyptian army of ten thousand men supported by tanks and fighter aircraft. For six days their advance was held up by the defenders of the kibbutz, a few hundred men and women with thirty-five rifles, half a dozen light machine guns, and a quantity of barbed wire, before the settlement was overrun. It was recaptured seven months later. Today, with the acquisition of new territory, Yad Mordechai is not even a border kibbutz. And the smoke that you may see drifting slowly over the few mounted sten guns pointing from a shallow trench at the tanks and figures in battle dress on the sloping hillside is not the smoke of war. For a moment Israel is at peace.

David Ben-Gurion reading Israel's Declaration of Independence in Tel Aviv Museum on 14 May 1948.

32
The Yemen Miracle

WHEN THE GATES OF Old Jerusalem clanged against the Jew after the second cease-fire on July 17, they were flung wide open everywhere else in the new state. In January 1950 Jerusalem became the capital, and six months later the Knesset passed the Law of Return by which any Jew had the right to immigrate to Israel. Soon the *kibbutz gaulioth* — the ingathering of the exiles — was changing the face of city and countryside.

Premier Ben Gurion told his parliament they were seeing the fulfillment of prophecy. He quoted Isaiah: "Fear not, for I am with thee: I will bring thy seed from the east, and gather thee from the west; I will say to the north, Give up; and to the south [the original Hebrew word was *teman*, or *yemen*], Keep not back: bring my sons from far, and my daughters from the ends of the earth . . . and these from the land of Sinim" (43:5,6; 49:12).

They had waited a long time for this to happen. But it had come about at last. Immigrants were arriving in different airlifts at the rate of one thousand a day. They were coming, as the prophet said they would, from China (Sinim, the old word for China) and from all other parts of the globe. They were coming because the bait of the Zionist had drawn them, and because the gun of the hunter had driven them. Many of them were coming simply because they had never forgotten the Book and its promises.

"Operation Ali Baba" brought in the Jews of Iraq — the oldest recorded Jewish community of the Diaspora, dating back to the Babylonian captivity. But they left Baghdad, 100,000 of them, only with the clothes they were wearing, and with a promise never to return. In "Operation Magic Carpet," 48,000 were airlifted from

Yemen, a little independent state south of Saudi Arabia. Yemenite Jews are small of stature, few weighing over eighty pounds. When conquered by the Muslims in the eighth century, they became second-class citizens under Islamic law. A Yemenite Jew was not permitted to ride an animal that would raise him above a walking Muslim; his house might not be higher than the house of a Muslim; he might not raise his voice before a Muslim; his dress had to identify him; and when he was, at last, granted permission to leave, all he was allowed to take with him was the Torah. Because scrolls of the Law were scarce, the Yemenite Jew was able to read a copy from any angle, thus making it possible for four or five to study a page at the same time.

One day the news got through that there was "a state in Israel," then that there was "war in Israel," then that "the proper hour had come" for them to return to Zion. The long exile was over. From eight hundred different points in Yemen they began to move toward Aden — the sick, the lame, and the women about to give birth, riding on donkeys. It took some of the convoys three months to reach the British Protectorate — where they were accommodated in camps on the desert sands with only the sky as a roof. Was this the scene Jeremiah had in mind when he wrote, "Behold, I will . . . gather them from the coasts of the earth, and with them the blind and the lame, the woman with child and her that travaileth with child together: a great company shall return thither. . . . Declare it in the isles afar off, and say, He that scattered Israel will gather him, and keep him, as a shepherd doth his flock" (31:8,10)?

The Jews of Yemen believed that it was. Many of them had never seen a plane before, but there was no panic when the great airlift started. They were merely flying "on eagle's wings" (Isa. 40:31) to their own land, where perhaps even the Messiah was now waiting. God had said to the ruler of a mountainous kingdom where time had stood still: "Keep not back," and by September 1950 Yemen was empty of Jews. Converted bombers completed what history has called "the Yemen miracle."

And the ingathering from seventy other nations of the world went on. Of the 1,600,000 people in Israel at the end of 1951, no fewer than 1,425,000 were Jews. A scattered people were coming together to rebuild the ruined cities and restore the land that centuries of neglect had turned into barren wastes. The prayer "Next year in Jerusalem" had been answered.

Only one problem remained — Jerusalem itself.

That it was a divided city had to be accepted. So had the intervals of firing across the narrow strip of "no man's land" that separated Israel from Jordan. These however, did not hinder the development that took place more rapidly and on a far greater scale in the western Jewish sector than it did in eastern Jerusalem. But while peace of an uneasy nature was maintained here, blood was being spilled on the southern borders of the new state, particularly in the Gaza area.

Farmhouses, schools, settlers working their fields — these were the targets of Egyptian raids. As a result of these and retaliatory strikes, the Jewish casualty list for the years between 1952 and 1956 was over one thousand either killed or wounded. The political scene in Egypt changed in 1952 with the exit of King Farouk and the establishment of a republic under General Neguib, with a former comrade-in-arms, Colonel Nasser, as the real power behind the scenes. Both had been captured at the humiliating surrender of the Egyptian brigade at Faluja in the Negev in 1948.

Two years later, when Neguib had been deposed and Nasser was Premier of Egypt, Egypt's attitude to Israel had taken on a menacing tone. At the end of 1955 Soviet equipment in the shape of MIG planes and Stalin tanks was arriving at Egyptian ports, and by October 1956 terrorist commandoes had penetrated as far as the outskirts of Tel Aviv. On October 25, Cairo radio called for a holy war against Israel; the armies of Egypt, Syria, and Jordan were placed under a unified command; and Egypt moved into the Sinai. After eight years the "second round" of the 1948 war had started.

It was to be as brief as it was dramatic. A massive retaliatory thrust in what is known as the Sinai Campaign brought Israeli forces to the Suez Canal in three days. Britain and France sent in planes to bomb Egyptian airfields and prepared to occupy the Canal Zone because of Nasser's nationalization of the waterway. There was urgent and strong reaction from Russia and on November 7 America joined the Russians in demanding an end to hostilities.

Four months later Israeli soldiers left Egypt. In their drive south they had captured Russian arms worth about $80 million and six thousand prisoners, each prisoner carrying an Arab translation of Hitler's "Mein Kampf." The two main objects of the offensive were also achieved — the destruction of Egyptian raiding bases and the acquisition of unrestricted access to the Red Sea port of Eliat, Israeli's gate to Africa and the Orient. It also silenced Gamal Abdel Nasser — for a while.

Mein Kampf *in Arabic, which was taken from Egyptian soldiers at Gaza in November 1956.*

33
Fighting For Survival

Rabbi Goren, Chief Army Chaplain, blowing the "Shofar" (ram's horn) at Western Wall immediately after its liberation by Israeli defence forces on 7 June 1967 (top); Israeli tanks moving across the canal to the West Bank in October 1973 (bottom).

FOR THE NEXT ELEVEN YEARS the Jews were left in comparative peace. They used that time to build their new University in Jerusalem, their Heikhal Shlomo center of the Chief Rabbinate, their Grecian-style Knesset, their pure white mushroom-shaped museum housing the Dead Sea Scrolls, their monuments to the memory of those slain in battle and those who died simply because they were Jews. For the living they built thousands of new homes and five miles outside the city, overlooking the village of Ein Karem, the birthplace of John the Baptist, they constructed a great new medical center whose outpatients' clinic now serves one thousand Jews and Arabs daily.

There was time now to drain the swamps of the Hula Valley and rejuvenate the earth, to bring water from the Jordan to the arid south. While the guns were mostly silent, there was time to sow and to reap. Where once there were no crops, now there was wheat and barley, and cotton and strawberries. Soon there was hardly anything, from chocolate to polished diamonds, that the Jews were not sending to thirty foreign countries. They were winning the peace as they had won the war.

But war again was getting nearer — for the third time in less than two decades.

On May 15, 1967, Israel celebrated the nineteenth anniversary of her independence with a distinctly modest parade of armed forces through the streets of Jerusalem. This was in compliance with a United Nations' ruling concerning weaponry in the divided city. But elsewhere, and at that precise moment, troops were on the move on a more massive scale. Egypt had decided the date was a good one to begin settling old scores.

While fifty thousand Egyptian troops, including an armored division, were taking up positions along the Gaza strip, twelve thousand Syrians were being deployed on Israel's northeast frontier. At the request of President Nasser, two days later United Nations peace-keeping contingents were suddenly withdrawn from Sharm-el-Sheik on the Gulf of Aqaba, and Egypt sealed off a vital outlet for Israeli exports. The blockade was supported by Russia, and, with the Arab world rallied behind him, Nasser, in a nationwide broadcast from Cairo on May 27, declared he was now ready to destroy Israel completely. From a station in the Old City of Jerusalem, Jordan Radio was telling the Jewish people that the "day of reckoning had come."

While the rest of the world believed that it had, 2,700,000 Jews were not so sure. Predictions of this nature had a familiar ring about them and these might almost have been an echo of the words of Asaph, the psalmist: "For, lo, thine enemies make a tumult. . . . They have taken crafty counsel against thy people . . . and have said, Come, and let us cut them off from being a nation; that the name of Israel may be no more in remembrance . . . they are confederate against thee" (Ps. 83:2-5).

Again from the distant past there was a voice speaking of things that were happening now. The skies were indeed dark, but history had more than proved that the "Jew was usually found standing at the grave of his enemy." As he had done before, he hoped for the best and prepared for the worst.

On June 1, Moshe Dayan, hero of the 1956 Sinai Campaign, became Minister of Defense in an emergency coalition Cabinet, and Israel braced herself for the new struggle — now only four days away.

Early on Monday morning, June 5, Egyptian armor (over one thousand tanks) attacked in Sinai; by noon, Jordan artillery was bombarding new Jerusalem and Syrians were shelling the kibbutzim on the northern frontier. In a lightning air strike that virtually decided the issue, however, Israel destroyed four hundred Egyptian planes (nearly two-thirds of the enemy's combat air strength) before they had left the ground. By Thursday, the main Egyptian concentration had been put out of action in the south and Jewish forces were at the east bank of the Suez Canal.

In the center, a tough battle had developed with Jordan for possession of the Old City. Tuesday saw all eastern Jerusalem outside the ancient walls in the hands of the Israelis and contact made with the enclave on Mount Scopus. On Wednesday came the historic breakthrough at St. Stephen's Gate and suddenly the temple area was in Jewish hands. That there were scenes of unashamed emotion at the Wailing Wall is not surprising. The strangely discordant notes of the *shofar*, the ram's horn trumpet (linked with the ram promised by God as a substitute for Isaac on Mount Moriah), heard only on rare occasions, was sweet on Jewish ears that June morning. The Jews were not only back in their land and not only a sovereign independent state; they were now in possession of that part of Jerusalem where Solomon had built "a house for the Lord." Miracles had not ended with the wanderings of his forbears in the wilderness, or even with airlifts from Yemen.

But the present crisis was not quite over.

The Syrians had still to be dislodged from a network of fortifications in the Golan Heights, from where for nineteen years they had been a menace to those in the kibbutzim below. Three solid lines of concrete bunkers sunk into the cliffs, barbed-wire barricades, and innumerable underground tunnels had to be penetrated. The struggle for this objective, according to one dispatch, reached a new level of intensity. But by Saturday the task had been accomplished, and the road lay open to Damascus, forty miles away.

Syria, however, hastened to join Egypt and Jordan in accepting the United Nations' cease-fire proposals, and the Six-Day War was over. Jewish casualties were around 700 killed and 2,500 wounded, with Arab losses estimated at between 10,000 and 30,000. Israel's gains were handsome. In less than a week she had enlarged her territory from 8,000 to 26,000 square miles. The flag of David now flew over the east bank of the Suez Canal, the Gaza Strip, Sharm-el-Sheik on the Gulf of Aqaba, Judea and Samaria (the so-called West Bank appropriated by Jordan in 1948), the Syrian heights of Golan, and, most prized of all, the Old City of Jerusalem.

On June 29 the Knesset merged the two sectors of Jerusalem into a single municipality and before the month was out Jew and Arab were mixing freely in the united city. Barbed wire obstacles vanished, walls that had divided were pulled down, all the gates of the Old City were opened, and the holy places of Christendom came under Israeli jurisdiction. For the festival of Shavuot, which fell that year on June 14, some 250,000 Jews streamed to the Wailing Wall.

Again Jerusalem had survived. And so had the Jews.

But six years later they were once more fighting for their life —
this time even more desperately than ever. Although Egypt had lost
two and a half billion dollars' worth of tanks, planes, ground-to-air
missiles, and other weaponry, by September 1969 Russia had
rearmed her. Nasser had initiated what was called the War of Attri-
tion for the purpose of softening up Israeli defenses along the east
bank of the Suez Canal and in November once again pledged his
country to the "inevitable battle" by placing 500,000 men under
arms. While commando raids were taking place across the canal, he
said that "for peace to emerge in the Middle East all Arab land must
be liberated — Jerusalem first of all."

But a year later President Nasser was dead and it was Anwar
Sadat who was to launch the next attack. It was three years in the
planning but when it came, it took Israel by surprise. On the afternoon of October 6, 1973, massive Egyptian and Syrian offensives
began, one across the Suez Canal and the other in the Golan Heights.
It was the most sacred day in the Jewish calendar — Yom Kippur, the
Day of Atonement, and Jews were nearly all in the synagogues.
General mobilization had been delayed and Israel's regular army of
some 11,500 troops were called upon to bear the brunt of the initial
onslaughts. No words, perhaps, sum up the position better than
those of Golda Meir in her autobiography: "The State was facing the
greatest threat it had known . . . only a thin line of brave young men
stood between us and disaster on the Canal and Golan Heights for
the first two or three days. But at the start they had no chance."[1]

The prime minister of Israel was not distorting the picture.
Ranged along the 110 miles of the west bank of the Suez Canal was
one of the largest standing armies in the world, comprising some
800,000 men, over 2,000 tanks, 150 antiaircraft missile batteries, and
500 front-line planes. The Great Bitter Lake separated the Second and
Third Egyptian armies. And at that particular moment there were
fewer than 500 Israelis in a series of fortifications known as the
Bar-Lev line on the east bank. Soon an artillery barrage from 2,000
guns, FROG surface-to-surface missiles, and point-blank tank fire
turned the front into an inferno, and within twenty-four hours the
Egyptians had established bridgeheads to a depth of four miles into

---

[1]Golda Meir, *My Life* (London: Weidenfeld & Nicolson, 1975), pp. 353, 360.

Sinai and fanned out along the entire canal. The crossing had cost them in manpower only a fraction of what had been estimated.

But where once the children of Israel had wandered under the leadership of Moses, there was fought between October 14 and 19 the most savage tank battle since World War II. More tanks were deployed in it, according to military experts, than in the British offensive at Alamein in 1942 or in the German attack on Russia in 1941. It brought the Egyptian advance to a halt, and from October 17 the tide began to turn in Israel's favor. By that time, too, a dramatic incursion on the west bank by Israel had brought her forces to within sixty miles of Cairo.

When a cease-fire came into effect on October 22, however, an extraordinary military situation had developed. While the Egyptians were then holding some 450 square miles of territory east of the Canal, their Third Army in the south was trapped between the main Israeli forces in Sinai and the Israeli task force of some 12,000 troops and 200 tanks that had penetrated deep into enemy territory west of the canal. An attempt by the Third Army to break out of its beleaguered position and recross the canal was repulsed, and another cease-fire came into effect on October 24.

Bitter and bloody fighting took place on the northern front. The Syrians launched their offensive with 1,400 tanks and during the first three days recaptured much of the Golan Heights lost in 1967 and advanced almost to the edge of the plain of Galilee. By October 10, however, the Israeli counteroffensive was well under way and in great armored battles 800 Syrian tanks were destroyed, and the Homs oil refinery — one of the largest in the Middle East — was set on fire. Tank and artillery battles of fierce intensity developed as the Syrians fell back to strongly prepared positions before their capital. When the cease-fire came into effect on October 24, Israeli forces were within twenty miles of Damascus and occupied some three hundred square miles of Syria proper. Almost their last success before the truce was the recapture of Mount Hermon's nine-thousand-foot peak (the place where some believe the Transfiguration took place) after paratroops and infantry had been flown in for a grim engagement.

Once again the battle had been won, the shopkeeper could go back to his shop, the farmer to his kibbutz, and the professor to his books. Once again the tourist could be invited to visit Masada and the pilgrim to deepen his faith in Jerusalem, in perfect safety. But

Jerusalem Divided (1948-1967).

this time the list of names between black borders in the Jewish Press was distressingly long. For the enemy's loss of 514 planes, Israel's was only 102 (50 in the first three days), but in human life the cost was 1,854 officers and men killed and 1,850 wounded. This was a sacrifice she could ill afford, but it was one she bravely accepted.

The thinking of many in Israel was changed by the Yom Kippur War. In her autobiography, Golda Meir confesses that she will never again be the person she was before the war took place, because she believes she should have "listened to the warnings of her own heart" and ordered an earlier call-up of the reserves. "But the world in general should know and Israel's enemies in particular," she says, "that the circumstances which took the lives of those killed in the Yom Kippur War will never recur."[2]

---

[2]Meir, *My Life*, pp. 353, 357.

34
The Bones That Rattled

Soldiers praying in a "sukkah" (booth) during the Festival of "Sukkot" (taberna-cles) at the Golan Heights on 8 October 1973 (top); prayers being offered in the Sinai Desert during the Yom Kippur War of October 1973 (bottom). So far, in recent times the Jewish people have won their wars. But has it always been in their own strength? Many would say no, but others would say that God does not take sides.

"YOU KNOW, I BELIEVE that when the guns stop firing you may get your Jerusalem." It was these words of a British Foreign Secretary sixty years ago that made the Jew feel he was back — after an interminably long time — on familiar ground. He was back where miracles happened.

What took place in 1917 recalled a far-off day when a Persian king authorized the rebuilding of Zion by a captive people in Baby-lon. The theme was the same; only the chief characters in the story were different. Instead of King Cyrus and his treasurer, Mithredath, and Ezra and Nehemiah and Zerubbabel, there was a man named Arthur James Balfour and a Russian-born Jew named Chaim Weiz-mann. It had seemed as if the heavens had suddenly opened and a Voice had spoken — the same Voice that had told Abram: "Get thee out of thy country and from thy kindred, and from thy father's house, unto a land that I will show thee" (Gen. 12:1). That had been four thousand years ago. A great deal had happened since then. There had been majesty and misery; there had been mystery, and from the beginning there had been miracles.

There had always been miracles, starting with the birth of Isaac, a son of promise and not of natural laws. In Egypt, in the wilderness, in the land of Canaan when he fought his battles, and in heathen Babylon where Daniel had prayed to his unseen God with his win-dows opened towards Jerusalem, there had been miracles.

Then for a long while there had been silence. There had been no thunderings from above, no revelations in the mountaintop, in winds that rent the rock, in earthquakes, or in fires. There had not even been a "still small voice" (1 Kings 19:12). There had been only the miracles of a Galilean that were not the ones they had been looking for. He had not delivered the people from the Roman yoke. They had not seen in Him or His works the promised Messiah, and He had died on a cross. Since then, it had been mainly persecution — not seventy years of exile, but nearly two thousand. But the miracle now was that they were still here, not only in the world, but back in the land to which they had never renounced their right.

Awareness of the miracle has not been lacking. Since 1917 the Jews have believed a great deal simply because they were told they were attempting the impossible. And they have seen the fruit of that stubbornness — or was it faith? Their modern prophets have told them that "all they ever had was a divine promise and an unconquerable spirit. But they have survived nineteen centuries of trial and agony and have risen from the grave to recapture a place among the family of nations."[1] This was perhaps the greatest miracle of all. In 1951 they understood only too well that "the Zionist Organization had reached an important milestone in its history, but not the end of the road. They had achieved a Jewish state, or rather the 'dry bones' of a state, upon which the flesh had yet to come."[2]

By 1967 the Jew in Israel had advanced a good deal farther along the road. The world had been confronted with a twentieth-century miracle whose significance, however, it had perhaps not even begun to understand. The speaker at the 1951 Zionist conference was right: a nation had "risen from the grave." And in 1967 it was possible to see that the "dry bones" had indeed taken on flesh and that life had come into a symbolically dead body.

What had materialized, in fact, was a vision that Ezekiel had in Babylon about 587 B.C. That great Hebrew prophet had been taken captive there nine years after Daniel and eleven years before Jerusalem was destroyed. He was married and lived near the river Chebar, the ship canal that branched off from the Euphrates above Babylon and ran through Nippur to the Tigris. Within a hundred miles or so was Eridu, traditional site of the Garden of Eden; Ur, from where Abram set out; and Fara, where Noah is said to have been born.

In this cradle of the human race God carried Ezekiel to a valley

[1]Emanuel Neumann in an address at the 51st annual convention of the Zionist Organization of America, 1948.
[2]Israel Dunsky, chairman United Zionist Party (General Zionists) in South Africa, 1951.

full of bones that were "very dry," and asked him if they could live. The scene, one of utter desolation and hopelessness, typified a people's desperate plight. First Ezekiel heard a noise, a shaking as the bones came together, then he saw the sinews, flesh, and skin come upon them, and finally, as four winds blew, "breath came into them, and they lived, and stood up upon their feet, an exceeding great army" (Ezek. 37:1-10).

In the divine explanation that follows, the prophet is told explicitly that the bones are "the whole house of Israel," which the Lord God would cause to come out of their graves and bring into the land of Israel. Here a new spirit would be put into them and they would know that God had fulfilled His promise. It was not a physical resurrection that Ezekiel had witnessed, but a restoration to nationhood. The cry of the bones, "Our hope is lost," is that of a physically alive but politically dead people. The bones were not in graves, but were scattered openly in the valley, the word *graves* merely symbolizing the Jew as being buried among the nations of the world. Resurrection to national life, however, is a prerequisite to spiritual life. The latter, if there is to be any sense and purpose in the whole history of Israel, must take place — sometime.

The location of the drama is significant. It is a valley, symbolic of humiliation and suffering. And when the vision ends, the bones are still there, but they are now standing upon their feet, politically alive, vibrant with the breath of national sovereignty. Only in the divine interpretation are they seen regathered, in their "own land," and there spiritually restored. But the two are complementary. Israel's national resurrection is a vital forerunner to her final destiny among the nations, and territorial security is implied in the vision, though not actually witnessed. All that transpires in the explanation flows from the essential fact of the dramatic spectacle — the resuscitation of the Jews.

The bones began to shake and to rattle towards the end of the nineteenth century as Zionism stirred the Jews' dormant longings for a homeland. In the wake of two world wars, sinews and flesh and skin came upon them, but only in 1948 did they "live and stand up upon their feet." In that year the Jews' long interment among the graveyards of the gentile nations ended. The days of their political extinction were over.

Nineteen years later, and exactly half a century after the Balfour Declaration, they got their Jerusalem, though not as easily as a

British Foreign Secretary perhaps imagined. Miracles there may have been, but the walls of the city had not collapsed. The prize had not been obtained quite after the manner of Jericho of old. And since then the brightness had begun to fade, with the future not so clear.

How long could the Jew go on believing that victory would always be his? And that lasting peace would come, if he fought hard enough, at the end of the next encounter? There was a limit to everything, even to his own inner resources. Nor had the Yom Kippur War helped. What it had shown him, and shown him clearly, was that he could never rest on yesterday's triumphs, never let down his guard. Was the sacrifice, the struggle, to be never-ending? What did it all mean — the call of Abraham, the possession of Canaan, the rise and fall of the early kingdom, the scattering, the almost ceaseless persecution, and now the return to the land where it all began?

The questions were beginning to pile up now. What was to come next in this strangest of all sagas? The wandering was over, but was the fighting just beginning? Had he exchanged one fate for another that was no better? His ancestors had complained that they had been brought into the land "to fall by the sword" and their wives and children to become "a prey" (Num. 14:3). Could the Jew be blamed if he had begun to show more than a faint inclination to repeat those words today?

It is best, perhaps, to accept the fact that the Jew is a mystery, and was so from the beginning. His whole history has been a paradox, like that of the city for which he has prayed without ceasing. He has been preserved because he was chosen; but his suffering has known no bounds. He had set before him the blessing and the curse, life and death, and urged to choose life (God, "for he is thy life") that he might "dwell in the land which the Lord sware unto [his] fathers, to Abraham, to Isaac, and to Jacob, to give it to them" (Deut. 30:19,20).

There was no lack of evidence that as the ancient Hebrews began their trek to a new country, they were acting in accordance with the divine will. Their odyssey was attended by continuous miracles, but they never ceased to complain. The bitter waters of Marah were made sweet, and manna fell from heaven; their "raiment waxed not old," and their feet did not swell during those forty years (Deut. 8:4).

A supernatural cloud led them by day and they had a leader whose like has not been seen since. But the complaining never ceased. Where were the flesh and the fish, the cool cucumbers and the green melons, the leeks and the onions and the garlic of Egypt? The people had been brought into the desert to die, they said. Their souls were dried up. So a wind from the sea brought the murmuring Israelites quails. But the Lord also smote them with a plague (Num. 11).

Then one day at Kadesh-Barnea, fifty miles south of Beersheba in the heart of the Negev, they refused to go any farther when they heard the report of the spies who had been sent into Canaan. "Would God," they had cried to Moses and Aaron, "that we had died in the land of Egypt, or would God we had died in this wilderness!" (Num. 14:1,2). And God gave them their wish. Of 600,000 men over the age of twenty, only Caleb and Joshua entered Canaan, "a land of wheat and barley, and vines, and fig trees, and pomegranates, of olive oil, and honey," out of whose hills, they were told, they could "dig brass" (Deut. 8:8,9).

What was also made clear to the new possessors of Canaan, however, was that they were not there through their own righteousness, for they were "a stiff-necked people," but solely because of God's faithfulness to His own promise. Does it matter any more today if there are those in Israel who have doubts as to whether they should be there or not? The Jews under Joshua entered the Promised Land under divine decree. But their occupation of it then did not usher in the millennium. So also the present occupation has not ushered in the millennium, but it has brought an era of conflict that has not yet the remotest appearance of being over.

So far, the Jew has won. But has it always been in his own strength? Many would say no, and others would say that God does not take sides. But did He not do so when the Israelites fought the Philistines and the Amalekites? Even before Esau and Jacob were born, God said, "Was not Esau Jacob's brother? . . . yet I loved Jacob, and I hated Esau, and laid his mountains and his heritage waste for the dragons of the wilderness" (Mal. 1:2,3).

The Jew still moves amid an aura of mystery, an object of hatred and a target for destruction, yet he is patently indestructible. In earlier days his enemies would not believe that he was "the apple of God's eye" (Zech. 2:8). They do not believe it today. And it is not always easy to see why the Jew should believe it either. It is far easier for him to believe at times that God gathered him "into the midst of

Jerusalem" in his anger, to be melted by his wrath in the furnace, like "the dross of silver" (Ezek. 22:18-20).

As yet, there is no ease in Zion. The Jews are still a prey. It is not yet time for them to "beat their swords into plowshares, their spears into pruning hooks" and to "dwell safely" in the land of "unwalled villages" (Mic. 4:3; Ezek. 38:11). Between God and Israel there is still a controversy, one concerning the Word that "was made flesh and dwelt among us" (John 1:14). And until the blindness of Israel over this truth is removed, neither the nation nor Jerusalem will know the peace and the glory laid up for them both.

35
The Next Temple?

The midsection of the southern wall, showing the stairway (left) that the worshipers ascended to reach the gates of the Temple Mount. Perhaps, some say, such a scene will someday be reenacted in fulfillment of Micah's words: "In the last days . . . many nations shall come, and say, Come, and let us go up . . . to the house of the God of Jacob" (4:1-2).

FOR A LONG WHILE the goal of Zionism was clear. What had not been so clear was the way it was to be attained. But that has all fallen into place. The Balfour Declaration, two world wars, four internal conflicts, and fifty years of pioneering have produced results, some even beyond expectations. A single generation has seen the promises that the Jew would return to his land fulfilled. *It was now possible to offer the toast: "This year, and always, Jerusalem!"* The long march through history has come, however, not to an end but to a new beginning.

Before even the end of the apostolic age Christian aspirations had soared beyond an earthly Jerusalem to a heavenly one. But Judaism, because of the Dispersion and centuries of exile, looked with an increased ardor and hope to the city in which the temple had stood. Was it not, in the messianic vision, to Jerusalem that the promised One would come, that here He would rule as a righteous King and from here continuing mercies would flow to all nations? Was not the city, one day, to be made "a praise in the earth?" (Isa. 62:7).

Possession of Jerusalem went far beyond its strategic importance. It was a portent, a sign, that the long-awaited kingdom was drawing nearer. The Jews have looked for signs since they were slaves in Egypt. Paul, who knew his countrymen better than most, confirmed this. "The Greeks seek after wisdom," he wrote to the Corinthian church, but "the Jews require a sign" (1 Cor. 1:22). Isaiah, proclaiming the great promise to the house of David, said, "The Lord himself shall give you a sign: Behold a virgin shall conceive, and bear a son, and shall call his name Immanuel" (7:14).

Seven hundred years later the first disciples asked, "What will be the sign of thy coming [return] and of the close of the age?" (Matt. 24:3 RSV). And they received an answer that could hardly have failed to satisfy their curiosity, even if it left them a little disturbed.

For it was a startling catalog of signs.

On the slopes of Mount Olivet, Jesus told them that the age would end in chaos, with "men's hearts failing them for fear"; famine, war, earthquakes, and pestilence would play such havoc that unless the time were shortened, all flesh would perish. There would be signs in the sun and in the moon and in the stars, and false christs and false prophets would themselves perform great wonders. And when there seemed no hope, they would "see the Son of man coming in the clouds of heaven with power and great glory" (Matt. 24).

There was another sign on this prophetic agenda — the Jew himself — etched in the parable of the fig tree. When its branches were tender and put forth leaves, this meant that summer was nigh (Matt. 24:32,33). The blossoming of Israel into a sovereign state was a sign that the kingdom of God was near. Ezekiel had seen Israel as dry bones coming to life in a valley. Jesus likened her to a fig tree beginning to bud. But in their last question: "Lord, wilt thou at this time restore again the kingdom to Israel?" (Acts 1:6), the disciples sought something that was not to be known — the exact hour when it would be established. With the return of the exiles, the fig tree has budded. It still has to bear fruit.

The Jews' patience will one day be rewarded. But Hosea, a prophet of the northern kingdom who saw far beyond the catastrophe of the first captivity, was not exaggerating when he wrote that "the children of Israel shall abide many days without a king, and without a prince, and without a sacrifice . . ." (3:4). That they have never known exactly how long this was to be is just as well. The knowledge might have been too much for them. But is it possible that "the many days" are at last running out, and the kingdom about which the disciples were so anxious is not now so very far off?

"We have taken the City of God," said Rabbi Shlomo Goren, senior chaplain to the Israeli forces, at the Wailing Wall in 1967. "We are entering the messianic era for the Jewish people." In his later years Ben Gurion declared that his people, *"standing on the threshold of the Third Temple would not be as patient as their fathers."* Was he suggesting that the time had come for the building of another sanctuary on Mount Moriah? Delicate as this question is, it is one with which Judaism must sooner or later come to grips. For it is cardinal to the concept of the messianic age, and Micah, for one, asserts, "In the last days . . . many nations shall come and say, Come, and let us go up . . . to the house of the God of Jacob; and he will teach us of his ways . . . for the law shall go forth of Zion, and the word of the Lord from Jerusalem" (4:2).

But the whole question of the next Jewish temple is as complex and mysterious as the Jew himself. Views vary on when and where it should be built, and even whether it is necessary to build it at all. It is held by some that the sanctity of the temple mount vanished with the destruction of the sanctuary so that the orthodox Jew's objection to approaching the site because he is no longer in a state of ritual purity is invalid. Again the orthodox believe that the temple should not be built now, maintaining that only the Messiah can do this when He comes, for did not Zechariah say, "Thus speaketh the Lord of hosts, saying, Behold the man whose name is The BRANCH [Christ] . . . he shall build the temple of the Lord; and he shall bear the glory, and shall sit and rule upon his throne" (6:12,13)?

While this would appear to be a sound basis for their belief, it does not preclude the construction of a premessianic-age temple, one that will exist during the cataclysmic period whose hard outlines were drawn by the greatest Prophet of all on the Mount of Olives. Malachi assumed its existence when he said, "The Lord, whom ye seek, shall suddenly come to his temple . . . but who shall stand when he appeareth? for he is like a refiner's fire" (3:12). Paul, in his Epistle to the Thessalonians four hundred years later, said that it will be in the temple that the "man of sin . . . the son of perdition," will sit, "showing himself that he is God" (2 Thess. 2:3,4). Jesus Himself said that "the abomination of desolation, spoken of by Daniel the prophet, [would] stand in the holy place" (Matt. 24:15).

While Antiochus Epiphanes, to whom this reference is sometimes applied, did profane the temple, he was but a type of the evil genius who will again desecrate the Jewish sanctuary in the closing stages of the age. It will be then, said Jesus, that those in Judea should pray that their flight to the mountains will not have to be made in the winter, nor on the Sabbath day, for a journey of a little over a half mile (the distance permitted on the Sabbath) would not carry them far enough from the turbulence that will then be in Jerusalem — a turbulence that will bring to an end the long centuries of gentile domination over the Holy City that began when Nebuchadnezzar laid its beauty in the dust in 586 B.C.

Is there anything to prevent a temple from being built now? If a prerequisite is that it must stand on the traditional site, then obviously there is — the very substantial Dome of the Rock. But this stipulation must be weighed against the words of Isaiah: "Thus saith the Lord, The heaven is my throne and the earth is my footstool: where is the house that ye build unto me? and where is the place of my rest?" (66:1). These words could imply that a temple has not been erected on the recognized site, and there are, in fact, other Scriptures that indicate imperfections in this particular structure. Everything pertaining to the former temples symbolized the person and work of the One who was to come; this will have been built without acknowledgment of Jesus as the Messiah.

Even if the sanctuary's siting is not considered all that important, there are, however, other matters regarding temple ceremonial that might at the moment prove insurmountable. All this is only too well known. At the same time, the capture of the Old City has made the construction of a successor to the ancient sanctuaries a tantalizing objective. The Six-Day War won the Jews an outer segment of what once made Jerusalem unique, but how long will the Wailing Wall satisfy a people radically concerned with their spiritual destiny? It may not be shouted from the housetops, but Jews know that something important is missing from the City of David.

They also know that forty million Arabs who could have passed through Jordan before 1967 to pray at the shrines on Mount Moriah must now pass through Israeli territory. Is it possible the Arabs could lose interest in the Haram area or be induced to transfer the mosques to Mecca? This seems extremely unlikely. All Islam believes that it was from the Dome of the Rock that Muhammad disappeared on a winged horse into heaven. So the Jew has guaranteed the Arab his right to worship on ground where the temple once stood, even though he himself was denied access to the Wailing Wall from 1948 to 1967. But it is also unlikely that Israel has resigned herself to the permanent loss of those thirty acres that were once the focal point of her existence. Just as the return to the land came about through a combination of singular circumstances, so, many believe, will the highly explosive question of the temple site be resolved.

And in the meantime, it seems, there is to be a compromise.

On September 17, 1974, just about a year after the Yom Kippur War, plans were launched for the building of the Jerusalem Great Synagogue, "the first large central house of worship since the destruction of the temple in A.D. 70," which, it is hoped, will attract Jews from all over the world. It is sited in the heart of the new city, next to the Heikhal Shlomo, Israel's chief rabbinical offices, and is to be capable of accommodating 1,700 people. Constructed of Jerusalem's radiant stone, it was to have cost $10 million. The launching date corresponded, and this was intentional, with the first day of the Feast of Trumpets in the Jewish calendar year 5735, and fund raising was parallel that in the time of Moses when every Israelite over the age of twenty gave a half-shekel to the tabernacle.

Although analogies are admitted, the sponsors have been emphatic that the project is in no way intended to imply restoration of the temple. Even so, some have seen in the venture a development of a highly significant nature.

36
"Valley of Decision"

The Plain of Esdraelon from the Nazareth hills with the town of Tel Adis in the middle and the mountain range of Gilboa in the distance.

THERE IS A GREAT triangular-shaped plain in Israel that breaks the country's central mountain range in two. It lies between the hills of Galilee on the north and those of Samaria in the south, linking the Jordan valley to the slopes of the Carmel ridge on the west. Napoleon once said that it was the world's greatest natural battlefield and John in the Apocalypse names it as the venue of the final conflict of this age. A scattering of Arabs who lived there when it was a malarial swamp called it the "Gateway to Hell," but it is today the richest granary in fertile Galilee. It is sown for thirty miles with wheat and maize and fruit trees and sugar beets — a testimony to the best in man — waiting silently for whatever time may bring. In Greek it is known as the Plain of Esdraelon; in Hebrew, as the Valley of Jezreel. And because at its apex in the south there is a strategic hill called Megiddo on which no fewer than twenty cities have turned to dust, it is also known as the Plain of Megiddo. Nazareth and Mount Tabor look down on it in the north and Mount Gilboa rises on its eastern edge.

The Canaanites were entrenched here long before the tribes of Issachar and Zebulun were assigned the area. It was here in the time of the Judges that Deborah and Barak defeated Sisera, captain of the army of Jabin, king of Canaan, with his nine thousand chariots of iron. It was also here that Gideon and his three hundred routed the hosts of the Midianites. But it was at Gilboa that King Saul fell on his sword after the Philistines had slain his three sons, and a heart-broken David prayed, "Ye mountains of Gilboa, let there be no dew, neither let there be rain, upon you . . . for there the shield of the mighty is vilely cast away, the shield of Saul, as though he had not been anointed with oil" (2 Sam. 1:21). Thutmose III, the mighty Egyptian king, said that his capture of Megiddo was worth a thousand towns. Through this valley have marched the Greeks and the Romans, the Crusaders, the Turks, and the British. Here, in 1948, the Israelis beat back five Arab armies.

On this site has been a long, sad pageant of blood and strife, and all but a prelude to the final storm when the kings of the earth and their armies will be "gathered together in the place called in the Hebrew tongue Armageddon" (Rev. 16:16). Armageddon is God's controversy with the nations. The nations will seek to destroy Jerusalem for the last time, but this battle will not be one the Jews will engage in on their own. It will be the day of reckoning for "multitudes in the valley of decision" (Joel 3:14), the day of vengeance on those whose wickedness is great and who do not know God; when the rider on the white horse will go forth to judge and make war, whose eyes are as a flame of fire and on whose head are many crowns. From whose mouth will go forth a sword and who will rule with a rod of iron; who will have "on his vesture and on his thigh a name written, KING OF KINGS, AND LORD OF LORDS" (Rev. 19).

One of the loveliest roads in Israel is the one that winds up from the Plain of Esdraelon to Nazareth, and as you gain in height, the now peaceful expanse of earth widens out like a rich tapestry beneath you. It must have looked something like this two thousand years ago. To the boy who was helping his father in the carpenter's shop the sight must have been as familiar as the street in which He lived. But the time came when Jesus went down to the lake and the river below and began a new life, knowing that all that would happen in the plain would have its climax in a city. And as the storm will break one day about the hill of Megiddo, so it will finally end in Jerusalem. When the feet that were pierced will stand again on the Mount of Olives and a people will look and, this time, believe.

Was it not Moshe Dayan, former Israeli Minister of Defense, who said, *"Next time it will be Russia"?* He could be right. The mountain waits in Jerusalem, and the plain waits below Nazareth. But the mountains of Israel also wait for the armies of Gog and for their destruction. They will come, Ezekiel is told to prophesy, "out of the north parts . . . riding upon horses, a great company, and a mighty army, . . . against my people Israel" (38:15,16).

It will be in the latter days when this enemy will descend on "the land of unwalled villages . . . to them that are at rest, that dwell safely . . . to take a spoil and to take a prey; to turn their hand upon the desolate places that are now inhabitated, and upon the people that are gathered out of the nations" (Ezek. 38:11,12). But this too will be God's battle. "Behold, I am against you, O Gog, prince of Rosch, Meshech, and Tubal; and I shall turn you around. . . . You shall fall upon the mountains of Israel, you and all your troops" (Ezek. 39:1-4 NASB).

Dayan's words portray the realist; Ezekiel's, the prophet. In the view of many biblical scholars, Ezekiel was writing about Russia 1,450 years before its historical rise, long before it was known as Russia. Only comparatively recently has the significance of his words been appreciated — as the shadow of the great power in the north creeps nearer the land that is now pulsating with life. The city of which God said, "I have chosen to set my name there," the city in which Christianity was born, is a natural objective for an atheistic power, for communism seeks to eradicate the name of Christ from the earth.

"We shall vanquish God in his highest heaven and wherever he seeks refuge, and we shall subdue him forever. . . ."[1] Deny God and you can remake human society on the lines of justice and equality ". . . the idea of God has always been an idea of slavery, the worst inescapable slavery,"[2] say the high priests of Marxism.

But what befell the Assyrian army of Sennacherib outside the walls of Jerusalem will find more than an echo in the destruction of the hosts of the "last Assyrian" to come against Zion. For seven months Israel will bury the soldiers of Gog, says Ezekiel. God said, "In that day, I will give unto Gog a place there of graves in Israel, the valley of the passengers on the east of the sea: and it shall stop the noses of the passengers; and there shall they bury Gog and all his multitude; and they shall call it The valley of Hamon-Gog. And seven months shall the house of Israel be burying of them, that they may cleanse the land" (Ezek. 39:11,12).

Is this history repeating itself on a vast scale? Was there a foreshadowing of this climactic event in a dispatch from Tel Aviv just after the Six-Day War when a correspondent wrote, "Israeli burial squads have gone down to Sinai to inter ten thousand Egyp-

[1] Grigory Zinoviev.
[2] Lenin.

tians killed during the headlong Israeli rush on the Suez Canal. Their bodies, putrified and swarming with flies, have been lying for almost ten days on the blazing sands of Sinai. Of the army of 120,000, only about 3,000 have been taken prisoner." A strange and striking parallel.

But Ezekiel discloses an even stranger detail of the future confrontation. Israel, he says, will burn the weapons of war for seven years "so that they shall take no wood out of the field, neither cut down any of the forests" (Ezek. 39:10). That these weapons are given as shields and bucklers and spears and hand staves does not limit the prophecy in time. These were the weapons of Ezekiel's day, the ones he knew. But weapons have changed. However, there is a problem: Would tanks and armored cars burn?

The Bible is its own authority in everything, but even in the light of modern science this statement sheds some of its apparent strangeness. For a chemically treated wood called lignostone is today being used extensively in cogs for wheels and in planes, tanks, and other articles of war. It is said to be stronger than steel, but is also elastic and burns with great heat. Iron and steel gather radioactivity; plywood reinforced with fiberglass does not do so readily. Could this be the material that will supply Israel with "firewood" for seven years?

Realism sees a day when Russia will move south against the people and the land of the Bible. But God has not called Israel back to her land to be totally crushed. The threat from the north will be met — as will the subsequent one of Armageddon — not by Jewish power, but by Him who promised, "Though I make a full end of all nations whither I have scattered thee, yet will I not make a full end of thee" (Jer. 30:11). Gog and his allies will be broken on the mountains of Israel as Sodom and Gomorrah were destroyed, an object lesson to the world. And "the house of Israel shall know that I am the Lord their God . . . neither will I hide my face any more from them" (Ezek. 39:22,29).

37
City of the Great King

DAVID EXHORTED MEN to pray for the peace of Jerusalem; Solomon built a "house for the Lord" on one of her hills; Christ died outside her walls for the sins of mankind; and from her ruined precincts a people were finally scattered far and wide.

But from Jerusalem now, after 2,500 years, the Jews again rule a land that was given them for "an everlasting possession" (Gen. 17:8). The long, tortuous road has wound back — back to where it began, at the spring of Gihon, the aqueduct of Hezekiah, the threshing floor of Arunah, the sanctuary on the sacred mount. The long road that went, it seemed at times, to the very brink of hell, and then turned suddenly to the City that had always been waiting.

Although Israel will never again be moved from her land, is it time for the kingdom to be restored? Is it time for a 1,900-year-old question to be answered? Are the words of Zechariah now to be fulfilled, for he said that the families of the earth will come to Jerusalem to worship the king, the Lord of hosts and that "ten men shall . . . take hold of the skirt of him that is a Jew, saying, We will go with you; for we have heard that God is with you" (Zech. 14:16,17; 8:23)?

One would hardly say so. Signs do not suggest that it is time for Israel to lay aside her weapons. It is time, rather, to prepare for war, for the rise and fall of the last great gentile powers, the sound and fury of a world in arms. "Ye have heard that antichrist shall come," said John (1 John 2:18). And so he shall, rising, in the language of the Apocalypse, "like a beast coming up out of the earth," having two horns like a lamb, but speaking like a dragon (Rev. 13:11). He is the

273

counterfeit messiah, the false prophet, the son of perdition, who will pollute the sanctuary and deceive the people, who will come in his own name and be received, unlike another who came in His Father's name, but was not received (John 5:43). He will have as his ally the beast from the sea with ten horns and "a mouth speaking great things and blasphemies" (Rev. 13:1-5). Together for a short while, they will ensnare and terrorize the earth by means of ungodly power.

Jerusalem will fall in a last, humbling capitulation before she becomes "the joy of the whole earth, beautiful for situation . . . the city of the great King" (Ps. 48:2). For He who was prophesied to be king of the Jews, who was born king of the Jews, who said He was king of the Jews, and who was crucified king of the Jews, will reign as King from the city that set Him at naught. The days of Israel's spiritual blindness will be over, for she will recognize the thorn-crowned One, and this time she will say, "Blessed is he that cometh in the name of the Lord" (Matt. 23:39). The bones that Ezekiel saw come together as a nationally resurrected Israel will be given a new heart and a new spirit.

Glory will return to Jerusalem. For this she was destined. For this she has survived since the humiliation of the Great Shepherd of the sheep. She must reflect the glory of the Redeemer who has come to Zion, for where He was mocked He must be exalted so that every vestige of shame is expunged. Where there was once a cross there must be a throne. Before Him who was reviled and betrayed every knee will bow. No triumph will compare with this.

It could not be otherwise. For John heard great voices in heaven saying, "The kingdoms of this world are become the kindoms of our Lord, and of his Christ; and he shall reign for ever and ever" (Rev. 11:15). Daniel saw the kingdom that would be set up when the stone (Christ) "cut out of the mountain without hands" destroyed man's last empire (Dan. 2:44,45). Isaiah proclaimed that its government would be upon the shoulders of Him whose "name shall be called Wonderful, Counsellor, The mighty God, The everlasting Father, The Prince of Peace" (Isa. 9:6,7). Jesus said that "when the Son of man shall come in his glory . . . then shall he sit upon the throne of his glory" (Matt. 25:31). Also the angel Gabriel, in the same breath that he told Mary she would bring forth a Son and would call His name Jesus, said, "The Lord God shall give unto him the throne of his father David; and he shall reign over the house of Jacob for ever; and of his kingdom there shall be no end" (Luke 1:31-33).

Jerusalem and the Jew must be there when the King comes back. On the Damascus road Paul saw Christ in His glory and believed. So, one day, will Israel. For her Jesus was a stumbling block. She could see only the Law and justification only by the keeping of it. And as a result of her blindness, salvation came to the Gentiles. Because of unbelief, the natural branches of the good olive tree were lopped off and the wild branches were grafted in. But the excision was never meant to be permanent. There will be a regrafting of the once-dead branches, a regrafting that will make the Jew a blessing in the earth and restore to him the years that the locust has eaten.

The great visions that Ezekiel had of the future included one of a temple — the one, it would seem, that will enhance the Kingdom Age, the one that the Messiah Himself will build. Its splendor will outshine the splendor of Solomon's temple, although it will have no ark of the covenant, no mercy seat, no cherubim, no golden candlestick. But the "glory of the Lord" (the Shekinah glory that departed at the time of the Babylonian captivity) will come into it "by way of the gate whose prospect is toward the east" (Ezek. 43:4). It will stand "in the midst of the holy oblation," a portion of land especially dedicated to Jehovah. Micah says that "it will be established in the tops of the mountains, and exalted above the hills, and the people will flow into it" (4:1,2). There will be no Passover lamb. Offerings will be commemorative and retrospective in character, looking back to the supreme sacrifice at Calvary.

A purified Judaism will be established and divine government will rule the millennial earth. "Yea, many people and strong nations," says Zechariah, "shall come to seek the Lord of hosts in Jerusalem, and to pray before the Lord" (8:22). The world will have entered the Sabbath rest day, the seven-thousandth year in Jewish reckoning, and the Apocalyptic thousand-year reign of Christ. And because its name means "peace," God will give peace to Jerusalem. Long before Israel was founded, and nine hundred years before David made it his capital, Jerusalem was already a holy city, because it was there that Melchizedek, king of Salem, and priest of the Most High God, brought out bread and wine and offered them to Abraham.

The faith of Abraham was counted for righteousness. He set out from Ur, the most splendid metropolis of his day, not knowing where he was going. "But," says the writer to the Hebrews, "he looked for a city which hath foundations whose builder and maker is God" (11:10). Two thousand years later John the seer, on the Isle of Patmos, saw "the holy city, new Jerusalem, coming down from God out of heaven, prepared as a bride adorned for her husband" (Rev. 21:2). Is this mystical or literal? Is it the place on which the patriarch had set his heart? a vision of the church as it enters its eternal state of bliss, or the actual, glorious habitation of God? Who can be quite sure? Except about one thing — that all will be perfect.

The magnificence of the millennial Jerusalem is here surpassed. The land in which Ezekiel's temple and city were located was bounded by the sea. But in the new heaven and the new earth there is "no more sea." And in the New Jerusalem, John saw no temple. He saw instead a city of pure gold, like clear glass, 1,500 miles square, with twelve foundations on which are the names of the twelve apostles. Its wall is of jasper, and the foundations of the wall are garnished with precious stones. Its street is also of pure gold. Its twelve gates, on which are written the names of the twelve tribes of the children of Israel, are of pearl. They will never be shut. And instead of a temple, John saw a throne.

When the Kingdom Age, which was not a perfect state because obedience to its Ruler was sometimes feigned, gives way to the Eternal Age, there will be no more pain, or sorrow, or death.

In Eden God walked and talked with Adam. During the wanderings of the Israelites in the desert of Sinai, He dwelt in the innermost part of the tabernacle. In the days of His flesh He was in the Word, "reconciling the world unto himself." During this Age of Grace, He dwells in the true church by His Spirit. But the supreme wonder of eternity will be God's presence with the redeemed of all the ages. He will be in the midst of those in the New Jerusalem and those who have access to it. "They will see his face, and his name will be in their foreheads" (Rev. 22:4).

Bibliography

Baly, Denis. *The Geography of the Bible*. London: Lutterworth Press, 1957.

Ben-Jacob, Jeremiah. *The Jewish Struggle*. London: Allen & Unwin, 1942.

Bentwich, Norman. *Israel and Her Neighbours*. London: Rider, 1955.

Bernheim, Alfred. *Jerusalem, Rock of Ages*. (Illustrations) London: Hamilton, 1969.

Besant, Walter. *Jerusalem: City of Herod and Saladin*. London: Chatto & Windus, 1899.

Blow, Desmond. *Take Now Thy Son: The Yom Kippur War: South Africa's Involvement*. Capetown: Howard Timmins, 1974.

Bright, John. *A History of Israel*. London: S.C.M. Press, 1966.

Collins, Larry. *O Jerusalem!* London: Weidenfeld & Nicolson, 1972.

Comay, Joan. *The Temple of Jerusalem*. London: Weidenfeld & Nicolson, 1975.

Dimont, Max T. *The Indestructible Jew*. London: W. H. Allen, 1972.

———. *Jews, God and History*. London: W. H. Allen, 1973.

Duffield, Guy P. *Handbook of Bible Lands*. Glendale, California: Regal Books, 1969.

Farmer, Leslie. *Land of the Gospel*. London: The Epworth Press and the Bible Lands Society, 1963.

Fay, Frederic L. *A Map Book for Bible Students*. London: Hodder & Stoughton, 1966.

Feinberg, Charles L. *Israel in the Spotlight*. Wheaton, Illinois: Scripture Press, 1956.

Frankenstein, Ernst. *Justice for My People: The Jewish Case*. London: Nicholson & Watson, 1943.

Gray, John. *A History of Jerusalem*. London: Robert Hale, 1969.

Grayzel, Solomon. *A History of the Jews: From the Babylonian Exile to the Present*. New York: Mentor Book, 1968.

Habe, Hans. *In King David's Footsteps*. London: W. H. Allen, 1973.

Haim, Hadassah Bat. *Galilee and Golan*. Jerusalem: Weidenfeld & Nicolson, 1973.

Heikal, M. *The Road to Ramadan*. London: Collins, 1975.

Hertzog, C. *The War of Atonement*. London: Weidenfeld & Nicolson, 1975.

Hull, William L. *Israel, Key to Prophecy*. Grand Rapids: Zondervan, 1957.

Hulse, Errol. *The Restoration of Israel*. Worthing, Sussex: Henry Walter, 1968.

Join-Lambert, Michel. *Ancient Cities and Temples: Jerusalem*. London: Elek Books, 1958.

Josephus, Flavius. *Antiquities of the Jews* and *Wars of the Jews*. Philadelphia: The International Press, The John C. Winston Co., 1907.

Katz, Samuel, *Battleground*. London: W. H. Allen, 1973.

Keith-Roach, Edward. *The Handbook of Palestine and Trans-Jordan*. London: Macmillan, 1930.

Keller, Werner. *The Bible As History*. London: Hodder & Stoughton, 1956.

Kollek, Teddy. *Jerusalem, Sacred City of Mankind: A History of Forty Centuries*. London: Weidenfeld & Nicolson, 1968.

Lapierre, Dominique. *O Jerusalem!* London: Weidenfeld & Nicolson, 1972.

Laqueur, W. *The Confrontation*. London: Wildwood House, 1974.

Lauer, Pierre. *Hussein of Jordan: My 'War' With Israel*. London: Peter Owen, 1969.

Lindsey, Hal. *There's a New World Coming: "A Prophetic Odyssey."* London: Coverdale House Publishers, 1973.

Loffreda, Stanislao. *A Visit to Capharnaum*. Jerusalem: Franciscan Printing Press, 1973.

Lowdermilk, Walter Clay. *Palestine, Land of Promise*. London: Victor Gollancz, 1946.

Luke, Harry Charles. *The Handbook of Palestine and Trans-Jordan*. London: Macmillan, 1930.

Mann, Peggy. *Golda, the Life of Israel's Prime Minister*. London: Valentine, Mitchell, 1972.

Mann, Sylvia. *Jerusalem, Judea and Samaria*. Jerusalem: Weidenfeld & Nicolson, 1973.

Maraini, Fosco. *Jerusalem, Rock of Ages*. (Text) London: Hamilton, 1969.

Maurier, Angela du. *Pilgrims by the Way*. London: Davies, 1967.

Meir, Golda. *My Life*. London: Weidenfeld & Nicolson, 1975.

Minkin, Jacob. *Herod, King of the Jews*. New York: Yoseloff, 1956.

Modiano, Colette. *Turkish Coffee and the Fertile Crescent*. London: Joseph. 1974.

Morton, H. V. *In the Steps of the Master*. London: Rich & Cowan, 1934.

Olson, Arnold. *Inside Jerusalem: City of Destiny*. Glendale, California: Regal Books, 1968.

Palmer, E. H. *Jerusalem: City of Herod and Saladin*. London: Chatto & Windus, 1899.

Parkes, James. *End of an Exile.* London: Valentine, Mitchell, 1957.

Paul, Leslie. *Traveller on Sacred Ground.* London: Hodder & Stoughton, 1963.

Payne, Robert. *The Splendour of Israel.* London: Robert Hale, 1963.

Peale, Norman Vincent. *Adventures in the Holy Land.* Kingswood: World's Work, 1964.

Pearlman, Moshe. *Jerusalem, Sacred City of Mankind: A History of Forty Centuries.* London: Weidenfeld & Nicolson, 1968.

Pearson, L. T. *Where Is Calvary?* Worthing, Sussex: Henry Walter, 1946.

Perowne, Stewart. *The Life and Times of Herod the Great.* London: Hodder & Stoughton, 1956.

———. *The Pilgrim's Companion in Jerusalem and Bethlehem.* London: Hodder & Stoughton, 1964.

Pfeiffer, Charles F. *Jerusalem Through the Ages.* Grand Rapids: Baker, 1967.

Porter, J. L. *Giant Cities of Bashan and Syria's Holy Places.* 1874.

Ramati, Alexander. *Israel Today.* London: Eyre & Spottiswoode, 1962.

Samuel, Rinna. *The Negev and Sinai.* London: Weidenfeld & Nicolson, 1973.

Schneider, Wolf. *Babylon Is Everywhere: The City as Man's Fate.* London: Hodder & Stoughton, 1963.

Scott, Walter. *Exposition of the Revelation of Jesus Christ.* London: Pickering & Inglis, n.d.

———. *The Tabernacle.* Goodmayes, Essex: G. F. Vallance, 1930.

Shanks, Hershel. *The City of David: A Guide to Biblical Jerusalem.* Tel Aviv: Bazak Israel Guidebook Publishers, 1973.

Smith, George Adam. *Jerusalem From Earliest Times to A.D. 70.* London, 1907.

Stanley, Arthur P. *Sinai and Palestine.* 1857.

Steckoll, Solomon. *The Temple Mount.* London: Tom Stacey, 1972.

Tatford, F.A. *Lands of the Middle East.* Eastbourne, Sussex: Bible and Advent Testimony Movement.

Unger, Merrill F. *Great Neglected Bible Prophecies.* Chicago: Scripture Press, 1955.

Uris, Leon. *Exodus.* London: Corgi Books, Transworld Publishers, 1961.

Vance, Vick. *Hussein of Jordan: My "War" With Israel.* London: Peter Owen, 1969.

Vilnay, Zev. *Israel Guide.* Jerusalem: Vilnay, 1972.

Wolff, Richard. *Israel Act III.* Wheaton, Illinois: Tyndale, 1967.

———. *Israel Today.* Wheaton, Illinois: Tyndale, 1970.

Wright, G. Ernest. *Biblical Archaeology.* London: Duckworth, 1966.

———. *The Westminster Historical Atlas to the Bible.* London: S.C.M. Press, 1957.

Index

Jerusalem Time Chart

B.C.

168	Antiochus IV (Epiphanes) desecrates temple by sacrificing pig on altar
167	Revolt of the Maccabees (or Hasmoneans)
165	Judas Maccabaeus takes city; cleansing of temple now marked by the Feast of Lights
141	Simon Maccabaeus captures the fortress Akra from Syrian garrison and city becomes wholly Jewish until A.D. 70
137	Simon succeeded by John Hyrcanus who builds up Jewish nation
63	Romans arrive; Pompey takes city and restores the high priesthood to Hyrcanus II
40	Parthians capture city and Herod the Idumaean pleads his case before Anthony in Rome
38-37	Herod returns to Palestine; marries Mariamne, a descendant of the Hasmoneans; and with Sosius makes himself master of Jerusalem after three-month siege
20	Herod begins reconstruction of temple on grand scale
4	Birth of Christ

A.D.

30	History's greatest mistrial and the Crucifixion
66	Start of Jewish war against Romans: martyrdom of Paul in Rome
70	Titus takes city after four-and-a-half-months' siege; third temple destroyed
73	Historic suicide pact of Masada defenders
132-135	Jewish rebellion under Bar Kochba; Jerusalem razed to the ground and name changed to Aelia Capitolina
324	Christianity becomes state religion by decree of Constantine
395	Palestine under Byzantine rule

614	Persian king, Chosroes II, lays waste Christian Jerusalem
629	Emperor Heraclius reconquers city
638	Start of Arab rule with capture of city by Caliph Omar
687	First Dome of the Rock build by Abd al-Malik
969	Under rule of Fatimid Caliphs of Egypt
1009	Destruction of infamous El-Hakim
1077	Seljuk Turks capture city
1099	City conquered by Crusaders; Godfrey de Bouillon elected first king
1187	Turks win battle of Horns of Hattin and Saladin takes Jerusalem without shedding blood
1229	German Emperor Frederick II regains city by negotiating ten-year treaty
1244	Tatar tribe called Khwarizmians from central Asia puts city to sword
1250	Mameluke period extends over 260 years
1291	Latin Kingdom comes to end with fall of Acre
1492	Jewish refugees from Spain arrive in Palestine
1517	Siege by Ottoman Turks when Palestine becomes part of Turkish Empire
1537	Suleiman the Magnificent rebuilds city walls
1799	Napoleon invades Palestine
1860	Jerusalem begins to spread out from ancient boundaries
1865	Palestine Exploration Fund launched to explore Jerusalem underground; city linked to coastal plain by telegraph; for first time in 1,800 years Jews in majority in city
1895	Theodor Herzl publishes *The Jewish State*
1897	First Zionist Congress in Switzerland

1890	Rail link from Jerusalem to Jaffa completed
1914	City's development halted when Turkey enters World War I
1917	General Allenby accepts surrender of city; Balfour Declaration
1920	Turkey renounces sovereignty over Palestine: Hebrew recognized as official language
1922	British Mandate for Palestine ratified by League of Nations
1925	Opening of Hebrew University in Jerusalem
1933	Arabs call general strike in Jerusalem where population now 135,000 (76,000 Jews)
1936	Arabs again call general strike; Britain appoints Royal Commission under Lord Peel; commission puts forward unacceptable partition plan
1939	Britain issues White Paper limiting Jewish immigration to Palestine; start of World War II; Jerusalem becomes a military headquarters
1947	Partition plan by United Nations General Assembly; Jerusalem comes under siege
1948	Mandate terminates; Ben Gurion proclaims State of Israel; War of Independence as five Arab armies invade Israel
1950	Knesset passes Law of Return; 48,000 Jews airlifted from Yemen; new immigrants from 70 nations
1951	King Abdullah of Transjordan murdered in temple area
1956	Cairo radio calls for war against Israel: Sinai Campaign
1967	Six-Day War: Jews capture temple mount
1968	Nasser initiates War of Attrition across Suez Canal
1973	Yom Kippur War and its aftermath; still no ease in Zion